Intricately Connected

Biblical Studies, Intertextuality, and Literary Genre

Heerak Christian Kim

University Press of America,® Inc.
Lanham · Boulder · New York · Toronto · Plymouth, UK

Copyright © 2008 by
University Press of America,® Inc.
4501 Forbes Boulevard
Suite 200
Lanham, Maryland 20706
UPA Acquisitions Department (301) 459-3366

Estover Road
Plymouth PL6 7PY
United Kingdom

All rights reserved
Printed in the United States of America
British Library Cataloging in Publication Information Available

Library of Congress Control Number: 2008931040
ISBN-13: 978-0-7618-4149-4 (paperback : alk. paper)
ISBN-10: 0-7618-4149-0 (paperback : alk. paper)
eISBN-13: 978-0-7618-4270-5
eISBN-10: 0-7618-4270-5

∞™ The paper used in this publication meets the minimum
requirements of American National Standard for Information
Sciences—Permanence of Paper for Printed Library Materials,
ANSI Z39.48—1984

In memory of my mother's father,

Rev. In-Sun Jun,

Who was killed for his Christian faith

By the Communists

During the Korean War (1950-1953)

Contents

Preface — VII

"The Lord's Supper as the Key Signifier in *The Da Vinci Code* (2006)" — 1

"Jeremiah 11:1-17 and Deuteronomy 29 Compared: A Study in Structure, Language, and Ideas to Elucidate Their Relationship" — 15

"Luke 4:14-30 and Its Socio-Historical Context of Galilee for Understanding Jesus of Nazareth and the Jesus Movement" — 29

"The Psalms of Solomon as a Pro-Zadokite Document: A Content-Thematic Examination of Chapter 17" — 49

"Prohibition Imperative in Septuagint Greek" 87

"Beloved as the Source of Redemption: Toni Morrison's Contribution to the Phenomenon of Scripturalization" 91

PREFACE

I began conducting a serious examination of genre and literary theory after teaching undergraduates at Brown University in Providence, Rhode Island, in the academic year of 1998-1999. In the course, entitled "Bible as Literature," which was cross-listed across three departments at Brown (English, Religion, and Judaic Studies), I encouraged undergraduate students to consider the interconnectedness of literature and literary consciousness across time and space. To illustrate this point, I wrote a poem in ancient Aramaic using the philosophical outlook of the Jewish Sages of the Babylonian Talmud. I provided both the original Aramaic composition and my own English translation. As there were advanced Judaic Studies majors, including a student who had spent a couple of years studying in a Jewish Yeshiva in Israel, some in the class were able to follow along with my original Aramaic composition. Using comparative literature methodologies, I illustrated to Brown students how culture can be deconstructed along the lines of literary consciousness that is passively inherited as well as actively acquired and of cultural "sharing" that can be artificially constructed at different levels.

My literary quest started in 1998 resulted in a fruitful breakthrough. I identified and coined a literary device, which I called "key signifier." I introduced my literary device to scholars around the world at the 2005 International conference of the Society of Biblical Literature in Singapore. An academic monograph soon followed with the title, *Key Signifier as Literary Device: Its Definition and Function in Literature and Media* (Edwin Mellen Press, 2006). This book contains further explication of the literary device that I have coined as well as research associated with literary criticism and film criticism. Many of the academic articles in this volume were presented at prestigious academic conferences around the world. And they are based on my critical assessment of all literature and art as intricately connected across language barriers, culture, time, and space.

Heerak Christian Kim
XIXth Congress of IOSOT
Ljubljana, Slovenia
Bastille Day, 2007

"The Lord's Supper as the Key Signifier in *The Da Vinci Code* (2006)"[1]

The Da Vinci Code by Dan Brown swept the globe as a literary phenomenon. Much has been written and discussed about the book. However, what is neglected is the impact of *The Da Vinci Code*, the movie made by Ron Howard in 2006, which is a literary/artistic phenomenon in its own right and even more of a broad phenomenon because the movie provided access to even the non-educated. In this paper, I will discuss the key signifier from the Bible–namely, the Lord's Supper–that is actively employed in the movie. I have coined the literary device of the key signifier at the 2005 International Meeting of the Society of Biblical Literature in Singapore as "a term or phrase that triggers a collective memory or a community value that is over-arching and all-encompassing. A key signifier functions aggressively in the literary context to spur audience to action."[2] I will show how an American movie maker drew on American collective consciousness to trigger the biblical key signifier of the Lord's Supper and the integrally related symbols of blood and fictive kinship that are inseparable from the collective consciousness regarding the Lord's Supper. In particular, I will discuss the visual imagery of the Lord's Supper painting and its association with other scenes in the movie that mirror and parallel the visual employment of the Lord's Supper. I would argue that the action sought from the audience is a type of fictive kinship apart from the institution of the church or religion.

The movie begins with the titillating scene of a murder in the Louvre. Jacques Saunière (Jean-Pierre Marielle), the curator of the famed museum, is

---

[1] This academic paper was delivered at the Bible, Religion, and Film Section of the 2007 International Meeting of the Society of Biblical Literature in Vienna, Austria.
[2] Since then, I have published a monograph on the literary device of the key signifier, entitled *Key Signifier As Literary Device: Its Definition and Function in Literature and Media* (Edwin Mellen Press, 2006).

killed by an Opus Dei monk, named Silas (Paul Bettany), after secret information is culled from the old man, who turns out to be the Grand Master of the Priory of Zion. The secret was regarding the location of the "keystone," which would eventually lead to the Holy Grail, which had been protected by the Templars for centuries and their modern successors, "the Keepers" or the Priory of Zion, since the Crusades in the Middle Ages. Although the old curator is shot, he lives long enough to write instructions for his niece, P. S. or "Princess" Sophie Neveu (Audrey Tautou), who is a cryptologist and an agent of the French government. The instruction is for her to find Dr. Robert Langdon (Tom Hanks), a Harvard University symbologist who is currently in Paris to promote his book. Unfortunately for Dr. Langdon, the French police Captain Bezu Fache (Jean Reno) misunderstands and misinterprets the cryptic text by the dying curator as pointing to his killer.

When Dr. Langdon is interrupted at his book signing and brought to the Louvre, Captain Fache tries to trick a confession out of him. Agent Neveu, being aware that Dr. Langdon is the prime murder suspect, helps him to send a decoy in the form of a soap bar embedded with a global satellite tracking device the size of a small button. As the soap bar travels on top of a travelling truck leading police chase away from the Louvre, Dr. Langdon and Agent Neveu find time to decipher the written codes of the dead man. At the end of their search within the Louvre, they find the treasure in the form of a laser inscribed key leading to a secretive bank vault.

Having formed a *de facto* partnership, Dr. Langdon and Agent Neveu embark from the Louvre, toward the American Embassy. It seemed to Dr. Langdon that the first course of action was to clear his name. However, their road was diverted when the French Police blocked the entrance to the American Embassy. Agent Neveu, driving her small Smart Car, pulls away and evades the police, binding them for the foreseeable future as partners-in-crime of sorts. Their first stop is the Swiss bank containing the safe deposit to be opened by the laser inscribed key that they had found at the Louvre.

Dr. Langdon and Agent Neveu correctly access the safe deposit box and find that they have discovered the keystone, or the map hidden inside a puzzle, that will guide them to the Holy Grail. As soon as they have the keystone in their hands, the bank manager, Andre Vernet (Jürgen Prochnow), enters and announces that the police are on their way and that they need to escape. Fortunately for them there was an escape clause attached to the safe deposit box because it was one of the oldest accounts with the prestigious bank. However, it turns out that the bank manager was out for himself. After driving Dr. Langdon and Agent Neveu to the woods, the bank manager points his gun at the two who were hiding in the back compartment of the bank truck. By quick thinking, Dr. Langdon manages to save himself and Agent Neveu, and they drive away from the woods, leaving the bank manager behind, shooting at them from the ground.

Dr. Langdon drives the bank truck to the chateau of his academic colleague, Sir Leigh Teabing (Ian McKellen), who is an Oxford don. Sir Teabing accepts Dr. Langdon and Agent Neveu into his home. The audience learns that Sir Teabing is an expert on the Priory of Zion and the "Holy Grail" they are protecting. Sir Teabing explains that the Holy Grail is not a chalice or a cup of any kind but rather a woman.[1] Specifically, she is Mary Magdalene,[2] who was the wife of Jesus of Nazareth. As proof, Sir Teabing shows the picture of *The Last Supper* by Da Vinci and argues that the disciple sitting next to Jesus of Nazareth on the left is not a male but a female.[3] In fact, she is Mary Magdalene, Jesus' wife, according to Sir Teabing. He argues that the two form a kind of mirror image of each other and that the ancient symbol for woman[4] – ironically,

---

[1] It is understandable how romance can figure into the idea of the Holy Grail since the whole idea of the holy grail originated in the context of Arthurian legends and romance stories surrounding them (Roger Sherman Loomis, *The Grail: From Celtic Myth to Christian Symbol* <Princeton: Princeton University Press, 1963>, p. 25; Jean Markale, *Les Dames du Graal* <Paris: Pygmalion, 1999>, p. 16). Although Joseph Goering states that "For all practical purposes Chrétien de Troyes must be considered the originator of the Grail legends as we know it today" (Joseph Goering, *The Virgin and the Grail: Origins of a Legend* <New Haven: Yale University Press, 2005>, p.4), Chrétien de Troyes's *Conte du Graal* has to be seen as having been influenced by and shaped essentially by Aurthur legends. Loomis writes: "The First Continuation of Chrétien's *Conte du Graal* the vessel is merely a magic talisman of plenty, whereas only in an interpolated passage and in later romances does it become a relic of the Last Supper and the Passion" (Loomis, pp. 24-25).

[2] It is important to note that human body parts could be a Christian relic as well as objects such as nail and clothing associated with the crucifixion of Jesus Christ (Justin E. Griffin, *The Grail Procession: The Legend, the Artifacts, and the Possible Sources of the Story* <Jefferson: McFarland & Company, Inc., Publishers, 2004>, p. 4). This shows the possibility of the "Holy Grail" being a human being or human body parts associated with the crucifixion.

[3] The tendency in *The Da Vinci Code* to point to the early rituals on which the Grail stories were founded follows the well established tradition of Hollywood, in such films as "Apocalypse Now" by Francis Ford Coppola and "Excalibur" by John Boorman. Martin B. Shichtman writes: "Despite differing world views, Coppola and Boorman both strive to return to those early rituals on which the medieval Grail stories were founded; they attempt to arrive at the essence of the Grail myth, thereby to capture its universality" (Martin B. Shichtman, "Hollywood's New Western: The Grail Myth in Francis Ford Coppola's *Apocalypse Now* and John Boorman's *Excaliber*," *The Grail: A Casebook*, edited by Dhira B. Mahoney <New York: Garland Publishing, Inc., 2000, pp. 561-573>, p. 561).

[4] Emma Jung and Marie-Louise von Franz argue that the "Grail realm" represents "the primal image of the mother, the wondrous vessel. It is so self-evident that this is a symbol of the feminine..." (Emma Jung and Marie-Louise von Franz, "The Central Symbol of the Legend: The Grail as Vessel," *The Grail: A Casebook*, edited by Dhira B. Mahoney <New York: Garland Publishing, Inc., 2000, pp. 149-173>, p. 149). Bob Stewart notes that Holy Grail literature points to the Holy Grail in personified human

in the shape of a chalice–is formed when the contours are drawn, joining Jesus of Nazareth's right side with Mary Magdalene's left side in the picture. After all the necessary explanations are given by the expert of the Priory of Zion, Silas the Opus Dei monk shows up. There is a scuffle and ironically the crippled Sir Teabing incapacitates him. And Sir Teabing's bodyguard, Remy Jean (Jean-Yves Berteloot) binds Silas up.

When the French police arrive at the door of Sir Teabing's French mansion, Dr. Langdon solicits his help by showing him the keystone. Sir Teabing plans an escape using his private jet. The jet is bound for Switzerland, but when Dr. Landon discovers a clue from the casing of the keystone that what they are looking for is in London, Sir Teabing redirects the plane to England. When they arrive, the English police, contacted by Captain Bezu Fache in order to capture them. Clever maneuvering by Sir Teabing, who hid Dr. Langdon and Agent Neveu in the back seat of his Rolls Royce, while the English police searched the plane, allows them to escape without much problem.

Following the clue, they go to the Temple Church in London. Soon, they find that they had been mistaken and that "A Pope" described in the clue referred to "A. Pope" or Alexander Pope. Thus, they go to where the poet is buried. There, Sir Teabing uses his gun to get the cryptext opened without destroying it. Agent Neveu does not have any clue as to which word would open the puzzle. However, Dr. Langdon finds the word ("apple") which opens the cryptext. Although he solved the puzzle, he does not let the others know. Secretly, Dr. Langdon opens the puzzle and takes out the map from the inside and then closed the puzzle. Thus, Sir Teabing does not know that he had opened the puzzle. Sir Teabing has his gun pointed at Agent Neveu, so Dr. Langdon throws up the cryptext in the air. Thinking that it still contains the secret map inside, Sir Teabing runs to catch it before it falls and the contents inside are destroyed. Sir Teabing almost catches it but does not, and the puzzle is destroyed.

Then, the police arrives. Captain Fache had traced the cell phone of Silas who was shot killed outside Opus Dei house in London, and he finds that the calls made to him by "the Teacher" was made by Sir Teabing. Thus, Captain Fache arrests Sir Teabing and lets Dr. Langdon and Agent Neveu go free. Now, with the map from the cryptext available to them, Dr. Langdon and Agent Neveu find the place, a church with the Holy Grail, which they have been looking for. When they arrive at the church, they find documents dating up to two thousand years, tracing the so-called bloodline of Jesus of Nazareth through Mary Magdalene's posterity; however, the Holy Grail is not there. "The Keepers," or the Priory of Zion, at the church welcome Sophie Neveu as the

---

terms as "the Virgin who bears the body and blood of the Saviour within her own body" (Bob Stewart, "The Grail as Bodily Vessel." *At the Table of the Grail*, edited by John Matthews <London: Routledge & Kegan Paul, 1984, pp. 174-196>, p. 174).

direct bloodline of Jesus of Nazareth and Mary Magdalene. Agent Neveu is reunited with her grandmother, and the keepers vow to protect her as her family.

Dr. Langdon goes back to France. There he finds out that the crypt containing the remains of Mary Magdalene, at least as thought by the Templars and the Priory of Zion, is present beneath the point where the large upside down pyramid point meets a small pyramid inside the Louvre. And the movie ends there.

On the surface, the plotline of the movie does not seem to emphasize the Lord's Supper. Thus, a question may be raised how the Lord's Supper is used as the key signifier. But this question itself highlights the nature and function of the key signifier in a literary text or media, such as a movie. The key signifier is a literary device with double trigger mechanism. First of all, the key signifier triggers collective memory using a word, phrase, or imagery. Thus, the semantic field of collective memory and communal value is called upon. But this first triggering is meant to lead to the second triggering. And the second trigger is the triggering of the audience to action. It is important to note that the second triggering is necessarily tied to the first triggering. Without the first trigger – that of triggering the communal value or collective memory–the second trigger is impossible. In a sense, therefore, we can describe the double triggering as logical in sequence. It is logical–although it may not be consciously logical per se–because the first triggering lays the foundation for the second triggering. Logical is a good word to describe the relationship between the first triggering and the second triggering because in terms of effect the triggering may seem simultaneous. In other words, as far as the effect is concerned, it may not be distinguishable in terms of visible time sequence. It may not seem like the second trigger happens after the first trigger; they may look as if they are happening at the same time.

This can be understood in terms of cognitive human process. Cognition may involve several logical sequences in the mind. This can involve several steps, and it is possible that the logical sequences are consciously registered in the mind. However, it is also possible for the logical sequences to happen unconsciously. Certainly, for the individual to whom the logical sequence is happening in the subconscious, the process cannot be discernible in terms of time. The process may be ignored in the conscious or may blend in together, thereby giving the effect that all are happening at the same time. An example may explain how this can happen. Take for instance the process that happens in the nervous system. The example of the nervous system can provide an analogous understanding of what happens in the double triggering of the key signifier.

The nervous system can be processed consciously. For instance, a person can approach a hot object. As he puts his hand closer to the hot object, he can feel the heat. Thus, he can pull his hand back consciously. His nervous system detects heat and sends the nerve perception to the brain. Based on the computed information, the person makes the conscious decision. But it is important to recognize that the nervous system does not always function on such a conscious level where the process is detectable in terms of time. In fact, most of human nervous response is done subconsciously. There are "instinctive" impulses that react to certain sense perceptions. Most of the time, these bodily responses do not register on the conscious level. That does not mean that they are not happening. And just because we merely see the result, it does not mean that there was not an input. We may not have consciously seen the input to the nervous system, but the fact that there is a response by the nervous system means that there was an input. In a sense, we can describe the process as logical. It is logical because without nervous input, there would not be a nervous response. For instance, a person's eyes blink because there is the nervous input that the eyes are too dry. Often, the person does not notice himself blinking. Sometimes, he feels himself blinking. But almost always, he will not sense his eyes being dry, which is causating the blinking by the nervous system.

The functioning of the key signifier can be understood in the same way. One may not always understand the conscious input that is producing the response. And one may not even "see" the response that is occurring as the result of the key signifier functioning as it should in literature or in movies. But that does not mean that the key signifier does not exist or that it is not effective. The job of the literary critic or a movie critic is to isolate and identify the process, much the same way a scientist will examine and identify how nervous system works, for instance in the case of blinking. The key signifier, like the nervous system, involves logical process. In the case of the key signifier, a literary device which I have coined, the logical process can be divided into two parts – or two triggering functions. First of all, the key signifier triggers collective memory or community value. Second of all, the key signifier prompts a response from the reader, the viewer, or the audience.

Because the key signifier as a literary device can function "subconsciously" or unnoticeably, it is not always easy to identify them. That is the beauty of the key signifier as a literary device. The key signifier, in this sense, can be seen as more like the literary device of foreshadow, rather than those of simile and metaphor. Simile as a literary device is quite easy to identify because all one has to do is look for is the word "like" or "as." Once you find these markers, you know you have a simile. Metaphors as a literary device are more difficult to identify because they do not have visible markers. Still, metaphors are not too difficult to identify because one knows that a metaphor is using a symbolic item to refer to an object, a person, or a thing. Thus, you know that the literary device of the metaphor is employed when the person or object being referred to is being referred to by term or phrase that does not seem to describe the visible or the obvious characteristic of that person or thing. The metaphor does not require any knowledge or collective memory or communal value. All that one has to do is focus on the term or phrase being used and ask the question: Is this term or phrase descriptive of the physical attribute of the object or person being described? If the answer is "no," then he knows that he has a metaphor.

The key signifier is far more complex as a literary device than the metaphor. Whereas the metaphor does not require any knowledge of community value or collective memory to identify, the key signifier necessarily requires historical understanding of the community to which the text is addressed. In a sense, therefore, the key signifier can be seen as truly an interdisciplinary literary device which takes seriously the advances in humanistic studies that have developed into the 21st century. In a sense, it is the first literary device of its kind in the post-modern era.

This post-modern literary device, the key signifier, requires understanding of the collective memory and community value of the audience. However, this is not enough. The knowledge of the audience has to be so developed that one needs to understand that what can trigger their community value and collective memory. Thus, unlike the simile and the metaphor, the key signifier is not bound in the text, in the sentence, and in the word. The key signifier is fluid and presumes the integratedness of communal human experience and cognitive process beyond a simple text, word, or phrase. It is crucial to understand the workings of collective memory and community value if one is to identify the literary device of the key signifier, effectively.

However, referencing of the collective memory and community value is not enough for a term or phrase to be identified as the key signifier in literature and movies. The key signifier as a literary device (which I have coined) requires double triggering mechanism to be identified. Something that only triggers collective memory or community value cannot be identified as being a key signifier. The double triggering mechanism necessarily includes the logical second triggering of a response from the audience. It is the identifiable response of the audience that points to a word or phrase as being a key signifier. In a sense, therefore, the key signifier as a literary device is highly functional in nature.

In the movie, *The Da Vinci Code* (2006), the Lord's Supper functions as a key signifier. The Lord's Supper as a key signifier double-triggers. First of all, it triggers the collective consciousness or community value attached to the Lord's Supper. And the second trigger focuses on soliciting from the audience a type of fictive kinship apart from the institution of the church or religion.

It is not difficult to understand the first trigger of the Lord's Supper as a key signifier. The Lord's Supper is firmly entrenched in the western consciousness as a communal experience. In fact, it will be difficult to find a westerner who has never been to the Lord's Supper, also known as the Mass or the Eucharist. Thus, anything resembling the Lord's Supper will necessarily trigger the collective consciousness and communal value. As it happens, *The Da Vinci Code* (2006) centralizes the Lord's Supper, thereby making it an aggressive key signifier, rather than a subtle one. In fact, the scene in the home of Sir Leigh

Teabing focuses centrally on the painting by Leonardo Da Vinci of the Lord's Supper and the significance of the Holy Grail.

It is no accident that the Holy Grail plays such a central role because it has captured the western consciousness as being special with miraculous powers as the physical evidence of the Lord's Supper. Many Christian pilgrims and soldiers have hunted in search of the Holy Grail over the centuries. Books after books have been written about it. Many movies have been made about it, including the parody, *Monty Python and the Holy Grail* (1975), which has become a cult classic. In fact, the audience is reminded of the great significance of the Holy Grail as Dr. Langdon tells Agent Neveu that nearly everyone in the world knows the Holy Grail. Of course, this is not true. There are billions of people in Asia who has never heard of the Holy Grail. The point must, however, be taken that in the western world, it is ubiquitous, and "nearly everyone" knows about the Holy Grail. In a sense, the movie's bias, in terms of the audience, is given away in this scene. This scene assumes that all of the audience will know the Lord's Supper[5] and its most famed physical object, the Holy Grail. Of course, this is true with the west but not with the east or the Orient.

This scene highlights another important fact. Without knowing that the literary device of the key signifier is used, the movie uses it. Obviously, since I coined the literary device recently, the makers of the movie may not be consciously aware that they are using the literary device. But this is the case with all literary devices that are coined and used today. It is possible to use foreshadowing without knowing that the literary device is being used. And it is possible to use metaphor or simile without knowing that these literary devices are being used. In the same way, it is possible to use the literary device of the key signifier without knowing that this literary device is being used.

It is important to stress that the makers of the movie made a specific point to show the collective consciousness and communal value of the Lord's Supper

---

[5] Even in the medieval accounts of the Holy Grail, the Eucharist is linked with it from early on. Richard Barber writes: "Even in the ordinary chivalric romances there is other evidence of this enthusiasm: there are occasional references to having Mass as part of the duties of a knight, or simply as an accepted ritual before a trial of prowess. But in *The Story of the Grail* the number of mentions of attendance of Mass is vastly increased, and this is true of all the Grail romances (Richard Barber, *The Holy Grail: Imagination and Belief* <Cambridge: Cambridge University Press, 2004>, p. 138). Lizette Andrews Fisher argues that Grail stories were used as propaganda literature in the Middle Ages for spreading the idea of Transubstantiation enumerated in the Fourth Lateran Council of 1215. Fisher writes: "For example, the miracles which were related as evidence of transubstantiation appear in connection with the manifestations of the Grail. The great change connected with the possession of the Grail is called its 'secret,' and the term suggested to contemporaries the words of consecration of the mass, words which effect transubstantiation, at that period called *secreta*" (Lizette Andrews Fisher, *The Mystic Vision in the Grail Legend and in the Divine Comedy* <New York: AMS Press, Inc., 1966>, p. 43).

and the Holy Grail because they knew that these terms/ideas are triggering mechanisms in the western world. In this sense, they unconsciously used the literary device of the key signifier. Furthermore, we know that the movie makers were using this literary device as a key signifier (even though perhaps unconsciously) because there is a secondary triggering. The movie focuses on fictive kinship apart from the institution of the church or religion. This becomes clear towards the end of the movie, where Agent Neveu is welcomed by her grandmother and the Keepers, who call her family. This family is a fictive kinship created apart from the church or religion. This point is further highlighted in the fact that Agent Neveu is not religious in any way. In fact, she is dedicated to a secular way of life, and one of the reasons for which she left her grandfather is based on what she perceived to be religious devotion on his part. The very fact that she does not care about her identity or anything religious makes her a good model for the fictive kinship based on secular ideals and separated apart from the church or religion. She indeed embodies the secular credo of politically correct inclusivity and radical tolerance.

Of course, the second triggering mechanism is further given significance in the fact that the movie points to Agent Neveu as "the Holy Grail." In the scene at the chateau of Sir Teabing, the host explains with laughter that the Holy Grail is not the chalice used in the Last Supper, but the crypt of Mary Magdalene, which was discovered by the Templars in one of the crusades and hidden by them until this day. Sir Teabing uses the painting by Da Vinci to show the ancient symbol of the female (ironically in the shape of a chalice) formed by the left side of Mary Magdalene and Jesus of Nazareth in the Last Supper painting. Sir Teabing argues that Mary Magdalene was married to Jesus of Nazareth and was present at the Last Supper. Dr. Langdon interjects and says that the mind sees what it wants to see, thereby creating some questions regarding Sir Teabing's analysis.

It is understandable why Sir Teabing's explanation is problematic. His main argument for arguing that the Holy Grail was the crypt of Mary Magdalene hinges on the picture by Da Vinci, many hundreds of years after the event. It is like saying that the Babylonian Talmud accurately describes the discourse in the Late Second Temple Period. There is a trail of missing documents that makes this claim difficult. Of course, towards the end of the movie, Dr. Langdon and Agent Neveu find themselves in a room filled with documents purporting to trace the genealogy of the posterity of Jesus of Nazareth and his wife Mary Magdalene. But we are left with open-ended questions, especially in light of the fact that earlier in the movie Dr. Langdon objected to Sir Teabing's emphatic stress that Mary Magdalene wrote a gospel of her own. Critically viewed, just because a document is preserved does not mean that it is authentic. That's the whole point of Pseudepigrapha and Apocrypha. There was a genre of writing at the time of Jesus of Nazareth that intentionally distorted facts and fabricated individuals and events as a creative exercise. We call such "gospels" and writings Pseudepigrapha and Apocrypha, and they are distinguished from other genres from the period that aimed at disseminating truthful accounts, such as the Epistles, the Gospels, and historical books. Since the movie is not an academic excise in genre studies or literary criticism, these points are not discussed. However, Dr. Langdon's passing comments throw enough doubt for the audience as to question the veracity of the so-called documents preserving the fact of the genealogy of the posterity of Jesus of Nazareth and Mary Magdalene.

Further problematic is the whole concept of preserving of the DNA to testify to the marriage of Mary Magdalene to Jesus of Nazareth. This is problematic on empirical grounds. First of all, it is necessary to prove conclusively that certain DNA belongs to Jesus of Nazareth himself. Obviously, this is impossible to do two thousand years after his life on earth. A piece of hair preserved, for instance, can belong to anyone. Any myriad of individuals may have had vested interests in claiming some hair to be the real hair of Jesus of Nazareth from the desire for profiteering to efforts to gain influence even within the church structure. In the same vein, proving that the crypt belonged to Mary Magdalene is just as problematic. How can they know that the crypt contains the body of Mary Magdalene? It can contain any woman's body throughout the two thousand years of history. Even if carbon dating "proves" the body to be from the time of Jesus of Nazareth, it does not prove that the DNA belongs to Mary Magdalene. Furthermore, finding the DNA of Mary Magdalene does not help identify the DNA of Jesus of Nazareth. Even if it can be proven that the DNA belonged to Mary Magdalene, that is all that it proves. Anyone sharing that DNA can claim genetic connection to her but not to Jesus of Nazareth. Thus, the whole idea of "Sang Real" or "Royal Blood" that carried down from the marriage of Mary Magdalene and Jesus of Nazareth is problematic from the beginning.

But in a sense, this problem is only ancillary in nature for the movie, since the whole point is to emphasize fictive kinship apart from the church and religion. The idea of a royal bloodline and its descendants who stand apart from the church and religion and undermines the fundamental foundation of the Christian faith is the point. The second triggering function does not necessarily require proof of the bloodline of Jesus of Nazareth. As it emphasizes a secularized idea of fictive kinship apart from the church and religion, the very notion or the possibility of the marriage of Mary Magdalene and Jesus of Nazareth accomplishes the purpose. The Lord's Supper is significant because it was the last supper for Mary Magdalene and Jesus of Nazareth in public among the disciples (according to the movie). It is significant because it points to a future of a secular society where there will be fictive kinship apart from the church and religion that fits the secular agenda. The Lord's Supper functions effectively as a key signifier because it recalls the collective consciousness of the audience and propels them toward the secular ideal, a second trigger.

Thus, the key signifier of the Lord's Supper can be seen as having two corollary elements; namely, blood and fictive kinship. Blood figures significantly in the movie from the beginning. In fact, the movie opens with the blood of Jacques Saunière shed by Silas, the Opus Dei monk. Later, the audience finds out that although the Louvre curator had been shot with a gun, he induced the blood-shedding and wrote directions in his blood on the floor for his niece, Agent Neveu, and Dr. Langdon to follow. Obviously, the blood shed to give direction is akin to Jesus of Nazareth shedding his blood on the cross to give direction for salvation to humankind. The fact that Jacques Saunière is found dead as if crucified on an imaginary cross with his hands stretched outward sideways reminds the audience about the death of Jesus of Nazareth. Of course, the "Satanic" symbol drawn on his torso makes him into an anti-Christ figure. But the point is taken that the scene reminds the audience of the death of Jesus of Nazareth on the cross. When the audience sees Jacques Saunière stretched out on the floor dead in that manner, the audience cannot but be triggered by the corollary element of blood belonging to the key signifier of the Lord's Supper.

In the same way that the movie opens with the blood of Jacques Saunière being shed, the movie closes with the blood of Dr. Langdon being shed as he shaves; in effect, therefore, blood opens the movie and blood closes the movie. Just as the shedding of the blood of Jacques Saunière opened a whole secret world, Dr. Langdon's blood in the hotel sink opens a whole secret reality. The crypt of Mary Magdalene, in fact, lay under the large upside down triangle in the Louvre Musuem. Thus, the symbol of blood functions as a powerful unifier not only of the key signifier of the Lord's Supper but also of the story and plot of the movie. Blood is like the two ends of the bookends on a bookshelf that brings together disparate but like-tending books into a one-subject-themed bookshelf. It is, of course, no accident that blood functions in such a significant way. Blood is an important ancillary element to the key signifier of the Lord's Supper.

In fact, the Lord's Supper, or the Last Supper, before the crucifixion is where the institution of the Lord's Supper was established by Jesus of Nazareth, according to the Gospels. In the Last Supper, Jesus of Nazareth holds up the chalice, later to be known as the Holy Grail, and claims that the wine within is the blood of the new covenant in his blood (Luke 22:20). Jesus of Nazareth exhorts his disciples to remember him by sharing the cup of the new covenant. Since then, Christians have held up the Lord's Supper as the experiential ceremony to affirm a fictive unity with Christ and with all other believers as a spiritual family. Since the crucifixion, the shedding of the blood related to the cup of the new covenant has been associated with the historical event to bind all Christians in a fictive kinship, and the blood represented in wine or the chalice, "the cup," has been the material evidence of the fictive kinship.

In essence, therefore, the two ancillary elements of the key signifier of the Lord's Supper can be seen as functioning together and harmoniously. Thus, the key signifier of the Lord's Supper along with the ancillary ideas of blood and fictive kinship functions to trigger the collective memory and the community value inherent in the west. This first triggering, in the context of the movie, *The Da Vinci Code* (2006), is accompanied by the second triggering of the audience to seek fictive kinship apart from the church and religion. In essence, the movie uses the key signifier of the Lord's Supper to redefine the goals for the community. In a sense, there is a subversion of the traditionally held values attached to the Lord's Supper, which is to bring Christians closer to fictive kinship with Christ at the center and with the church as the primary earthly reference point for such a fictive kinship. Of course, the success of the key signifier is hard to quantify. However, the double triggering or the function of the key signifier in the movie can be identified. With time, it may be possible to assess the success of the intended functions of the key signifier of the Lord's Supper employed (albeit subversively) by the film.

Bibliography

Barber, Richard. *The Holy Grail: Imagination and Belief.* Cambridge: Harvard University Press, 2004.

Baudry, Robert. *Graal et literatures d'aujourd'hui.* Rennes: Terre de Brume Éditions, 1998.

Bayer, Hans. *Gral: Die Hochmittelalterliche Glaubenskrise im Spiegel der Literature.* Stuttgart: Anton Hiersemann, 1983.

Bryant, Nigel (Translator). *The Legend of the Grail.* Cambridge: D. S. Brewer, 2004.

Burdach, Konrad. *Der Gral: Forschungen über seinen Ursprung und seinen Zusammenhang mit der Longinuslegende.* Darmstadt: Wissenschaftliche Buchgesellschaft, 1974.

Combes, Annie, and Annie Bertin. *Écritures du Graal.* Paris: Presses Universitaires de France, 2001.

Ermarth, Elizabeth Deeds. *The English Novel in History 1840-1895.* London: Routledge, 1997.

Evola, Julius. *Das Mysterium des Grals.* München-Planegg: Otto Wilhelm Barth-Verlag GMBH, 1955.

Fisher, Lizette Andrews. *The Mystic Vision in the Grail and in The Divine Comedy.* New York: AMS Press, Inc., 1966.

Goering, Joseph. *The Virgin and the Grail: Origins of a Legend.* New Haven: Yale University Press, 2005.

Griffin, Justin E. *The Grail Procession: The Legend, the Artifacts, and the Possible Sources of the Story.* Jefferson: McFarland & Company, Inc., Publishers, 2004.

Hunt, Peter, and Millicent Lenz. *Alternative Worlds in Fantasy Fiction.* London: Continuum, 2001.

Irwin, W. R. *The Game of the Impossible: A Rhetoric of Fantasy.* Urbana: University of Illinois Press, 1976.

Keith, W. J. *Region of the Imagination: The Development of British Rural Fiction.* Toronto: University of Toronto Press, 1988.

Knight, Mark, and Thomas Woodman. *Biblical Religion and the Novel, 1700-2000.* Aldershot: Ashgate, 2006.

Loomis, Roger Sherman. *The Grail: From Celtic Myth to Christian Symbol*. Princeton: Princeton University Press, 1963.

Mahoney, Dhira B. (Editor). *The Grail: A Casebook*. New York: Garland Publishing, Inc., 2000.

Manlove, C. N. *Modern Fantasy: Five Studies*. Cambridge: Cambridge University Press, 1975.

Manlove, C. N. *The Impulse of Fantasy Literature*. Kent: The Kent State University Press, 1983.

Markale, Jean. *Les Dames du Graal*. Paris: Pygmalion, 1999.

Matthews, John (Editor). *At the Table of the Grail: Magic & the Use of Imagination*. London: Routledge & Kegan Paul, 1984.

Morse, Donald E., Marshall B. Tymn, and Csilla Bertha (Editors). *The Celebration of the Fantastic: Selected Papers from the Tenth Anniversary International Conference on the Fantastic in the Arts*. Westport: Greenwood Press, 1992.

Nelli, René. *Lumière du Graal: Études et Textes*. Paris: Les Cahiers du Sud, 1951.

Potter, Jonathan, Peter Stringer, and Margaret Wetherell. *Social Texts and Context: Literature and Social Psychology*. London: Routledge & Kegan Paul, 1984.

Varnado, S. L. *Haunted Presence: The Numinous in Gothic Fiction*. Tuscaloosa: The University of Alabama Press, 1987.

Wiesenfarth, Joseph. *Gothic Manners and the Classic English Novel*. Madison: The University of Wisconsin Press, 1988.

"Jeremiah 11:1-17 and Deuteronomy 29 Compared: A Study in Structure, Language, and Ideas to Elucidate Their Relationship"

Scholars of Jeremiah have often asked the question about the relationship between the book of Jeremiah and the book of Deuteronomy. Scholars have posited the relationship in terms of (1) Deuteronomy influencing Jeremiah,[1] (2) Jeremiah influencing Deuteronomy,[2] and (3) Deuteronomy and Jeremiah being influenced by a common source.[3] There are many reasons why scholars have posited a close connection between Jeremiah and Deuteronomy. First of all, the date of Jeremiah[4] coincides with the discovery of the book of

---

[1] E. W. Nicholson, *Preaching to the Exiles: A Study of the Prose Tradition in the Book of Jeremiah* (Oxford: Basil Blackwell, 1970), pp. 124-126. Artur Weiser, *Das Buch Jeremia* (Göttingen: Vandenhoeck & Ruprecht, 1969).
[2] J. Philip Hyatt, "Jeremiah and Deuteronomy," *A Prophet to the Nations: Essays in Jeremiah Studies*, ed. Leo G. Perdue and Brian W. Kovacs (Winona Lake: Eisenbrauns, 1984, pp. 113-127), pp. 113, 126-127.
[3] Robert P. Carroll emphasizes Deuteronomistic composition of Deuteronomy and Deuteronomistic editing of the book of Jeremiah (*From Chaos to Covenant: Uses of Prophecy in the Book of Jeremiah* <London: SCM Press Ltd, 1981>, pp. 13-14). See Robert P. Carroll's commentary on Jeremiah. Mark Ancace lists Jeremiah 11:1-13 as one of the texts in Jeremiah that shows a strong Deuteronomistic trace (*Jeremiah, Zekekiah and the Fall of Jerusalem* <New York: T. & T. Clark, 2005>, p. 20).
[4] John L. Mackay writes: "The prophet's fate anticipatively mirrors that of his people. By spurning Jeremiah as the LORD's prophet the community brings upon itself the suffering of the people rejected by the LORD, just as the prophet had already known suffering through their rejection of his mission" (*Jeremiah: An Introduction and Commentary (Volume 1: Chapters 1-20)* <Fearn: Mentor, 2004>, p. 393). Martin Buber also states that Jeremiah's " 'I' is so deeply set in the 'I' of the people that his life cannot be regarded as that of an individual" (*The Prophetic Faith*, trans. Carlyle Witton-Davies <New York: Harper and Row, 1949>, p. 181). Timothy Polk describes Jeremiah as "a paradigm" (*The Prophetic Persona: Jeremiah and the Language of the Self* <Sheffield: JSOT Press, 1984>, p. 170).

Deuteronomy[5] by King Josiah and the ensuing reforms[6] based on Deuteronomic principles.[7] Second of all, there seems to be similarity in language between the two books and some scholars feel that the similarities in language are stark enough to posit a direct influence (or commonality of influence). Thirdly, there is theological congruence on many points. Some scholars point to the strong commonality in ideas to posit that there was direct influence.

In this study, I will investigate the relationship between Jeremiah and Deuteronomy by comparing Jeremiah 11:1-17 with Deuteronomy 29. I would like to argue that there is a direct connection between Jeremiah 11:1-17 and Deuteronomy 29. Studying of the structure, language, and ideas of Jeremiah 11:1-17 and Deuteronomy 29 shows that that Jeremiah 11:1-17 is dependent on Deuteronomy 29.

First, we will examine the structure of Jeremiah 11:1-17 and Deuteronomy 29. This block of Jeremiah begins with the prophetic formula: "This is the word that came to Jeremiah from the LORD" (Jeremiah 11:1). We see that the prophetic formula indicates that God has given prophecy to Jeremiah, and this prophecy is being narrated by a third person narrator. When we compare this prophetic formula to the formula in Deuteronomy 29, we find similarities. Deuteronomy 29:1 states: "These are the terms of the covenant the LORD commanded Moses to make with the Israelites." We see here that it is the same structure. God is giving "prophecy" to Moses, and this "prophecy" is being reported by a third person narrator. It is important to note that the Hebrew word דבר is used in both instances. It is significant that the structure of the prologue is essentially the same in Jeremiah 11:1-17 and Deuteronomy 29.

There is a difference, however, and it is significant enough to be noted. In Jeremiah 11:1-17, much of the prophetic material is delivered by God to Jeremiah. Thus, God is speaking and Jeremiah is listening. However, in Deuteronomy 29, we see that the divine material is delivered by Moses to all the Israelites who have been summoned (Deuteronomy 29:2 [MT 29:1]). Although

---

[5] See Marvin A. Sweeney, *King Josiah of Judah: The Lost Messiah of Israel* (New York: Oxford University Press, 2001), pp. 137, 139.

[6] Josianic reform is dated to 621 BC and the beginning of Jeremiah's ministry to 611 BC (Josef Schreiner, "Jeremia und die joschijanische Reform: Probleme-Fragen-Antworten," *Jeremia und die »deuteronomistische Bewegung«*, ed. Walter Groß <Weinheim: Beltz Athenäum Verlag, 1995, pp. 11-31>, p. 14).

[7] Jeremiah's prophetic ministry spanned from 627-580 BC. Philip J. King writes: "It is an especially well known era of biblical history. A wealth of archaeological remains and extant texts, both biblical and nonbiblical, makes it possible to reconstruct the historical and political background of the late seventh century B.C.E. Archaeological discoveries from excavations and surveys conducted since 1970 are providing fresh data. Several sites with seventh-century artefacts, including Lachish, Beer-Sheba, Arad, and Engedi, have already been excavated. During the seventh century B.C.E., new towns, including Tel 'Ira, Tel 'Aroer, Tel Masos, and Tel Malhata, flourished in the Negev (*Jeremiah: An Archaeological Companion* <Louisville: Westminster/John Knox Press, 1993>, p. 14).

some may make the case that this is structurally a significant factor, I would argue that it is not as significant as it may appear on the surface. I argue this point based on the fact that the divine speech in Jeremiah was meant to be delivered.[8] Thus, there is the assumption that the prophetic speech in the mouth of God would have been faithfully delivered verbatim to the people. Secondly, although we are discussing structural issues, we have to take into consideration the content of the message. The message in Jeremiah 11:1-17 is a message about the destruction of Israel and Judah. There is the idea that the covenant was broken and thus the covenantal relationship between God and Israelites is no longer in effect. Given the seriousness of the message, a more direct divine formula is used. Thus, the difference is explainable based on content. More will be discussed later on this.

There are further structural similarities between Jeremiah 11:1-17 and Deuteronomy 29. When we look at Jeremiah 11:1-17, we see two blocks of materials which are synonymous or analogous repetitions; namely, Jeremiah 11:3-5 and Jeremiah 11:6-8. Jeremiah 11:3-5 basically recalls Egypt and the covenant.[9] God demands that the covenant be fulfilled and if it is, then he would fulfil his part. In this block, that would be (1) God will be their God and (2) God will fulfil the oath by giving the promised land. The implication is that God will not fulfil his part of the covenant if Israelites do not keep their part of the covenant.

Similar idea is found in the second block of Jeremiah 11:1-17. We see that Jeremiah 11:6-8 has a corresponding framework structure; it recalls Egypt and the covenant. Like Jeremiah 11:3-5, there is a demand for fulfilling the covenant. Thus, the two blocks function synonymously to enforce the covenant recalling Egypt. However, there is a difference. The second block emphasizes that the covenant was broken. As a result, God brought down the curses of the covenant.

When we look at Deuteronomy 29, there is a similar type of two-block structure functioning. Like Jeremiah 11:1-17, there are two analogous blocks in Deuteronomy 29; namely, Deuteronomy 29:2-15 [MT 29:1-14] and Deuteronomy 29:16-21 [MT 29:15-20]. And like the first two large blocks in Jeremiah 11:1-17, the first two large blocks in Deuteronomy 29 recall Egypt and the covenant. Interestingly enough, the relationship between the two blocks in Deuteronomy 29 correspond to the two blocks of Jeremiah 11 in terms of order. Deuteronomy 29:2-15 [MT 29:1-14] recalls Egypt and calls on the Israelites to

---

[8] Kelvin G. Friebel writes: "In Jeremiah, the language commanding verbal pronouncement is clearly indicated by דבר ... קרא ... אמר ... and נגד " *Jeremiah's and Ezekiel's Sign-Acts* <Sheffield: Sheffield Academic Press, 1999>, p. 33).

[9] Antti Laato states: "The exodus tradition and covenant theology are closely interconnected in Jer" (*History and Ideology in the Old Testament Prophetic Literature: A Semiotic Approach to the Reconstruction of the Proclamation of the Historical Prophets* <Stockholm: Almqwist & Wiksell International, 1996>, p. 259).

fulfil their covenant to God. Furthermore, God promises that if they keep their part of the covenant, (1) God will be their God and (2) God will give them the promised land. One can see that the first large block of Deuteronomy 29 corresponds to the first large block of Jeremiah 11:1-17.

Likewise, the second block of Deuteronomy 29 corresponds to the second block of Jeremiah 11:1-17. Deuteronomy 29:16-21 [MT 29:15-20] recalls Egypt and the covenant. Like the second block in Jeremiah, the second block in Deuteronomy demands observing of the covenant. There is similarity beyond this. Just as the second block in Jeremiah calls down the curses of the covenant for violation of the covenant, the second block of Deuteronomy calls down the curses of the covenant for the violation of the covenant. The only difference is that the Deuteronomy block singles out the violator of the covenant and explains that he will be singled out for the curses of the covenant, whereas in the Jeremiah block, it seems that all will be punished. In other words, there is a corporate communal punishment emphasis in Jeremiah. But to limit oneself to this surface reading may not be doing the text in Deuteronomy justice. When one reads a little bit further on (Deuteronomy 29:22-24 [MT 29:21-23]), one sees that there is an emphasis on corporate punishment for covenant violation in Deuteronomy 29 like in Jeremiah 11:1-17.

Similarities between Jeremiah and Deuteronomy do not stop with the two blocks. I would argue that the final block (the third large block) in both of the passages correspond to each other. Jeremiah 11:9-17 corresponds to Deuteronomy 29:22-29 (MT 29:22-28). Both sections have the structure that incorporates the accusation and the punishment. In Jeremiah 11:9-17, the accusation comes first and then the punishment, which is total devastation. In Deuteronomy 29:22-29 (MT 29:21-28), the passage starts with the punishment and then lists the accusation. Although the order of the two main elements is reversed, we can see that the framework structure of the block embodies accusation-punishment.

There are some notable differences between the third blocks in the two passages. Jeremiah 11:9-17 does not mention Egypt explicitly, but Deuteronomy 29:22-29 (MT 29:21-28) does. However, although the name Egypt may be omitted in Jeremiah, the implication is there. This implication exists on the force of the two blocks of materials in Jeremiah that preceded this block, which specifically mentioned Egypt. Furthermore, the mention of the forefathers in Jeremiah 11:10 recalls the name of Egypt. However, the reason why Egypt is specifically not mentioned is that Jeremiah wants to include the idea that not only the covenant at the time of Egypt but also the Abrahamic covenant is included.

Another notable difference is that in Jeremiah 11:9-17, there are two places where God mentions explicitly the idea that he will refuse to answer the prayers (verses 11 and 14). Although this does not seem to appear within the structure of Deuteronomy 29:22-29 [MT 29:21-28], the idea is implicitly found in the previous block in verses 19-20 [MT verses 18-19] of Deuteronomy 29. The explicit refusal to answer prayers can be seen as a significant structural difference between Jeremiah 11:9-17 and Deuteronomy 29:22-29, as it is visibly missing in Deuteronomy 29. However, in the context of the mega-structure of Deuteronomy 29 and Jeremiah 11:1-17, the idea–however implicit–exists in both passages (cf. Deuteronomy 29:20 [MT 29:19]).

Further difference between Deuteronomy 29:22-29 [MT 29:21-28] and Jeremiah 11:9-17 can be seen in the fact that the block in Deuteronomy develops the idea of destruction much more fully (Deuteronomy 29:23 [MT 29:22]). The devastated land will be a burning waste like that of Sodom and Gomorrah, Admah and Zeboiim. The indication is that the land will be completely wasted and the inhabitants killed. Jeremiah 11:9-17 seems to be far milder in comparison due to lack of graphic, detailed description. The Jeremiah block mentions only disaster in a general sense (רעה in verses 11, 12, and 17). However, a section in Jeremiah does recall the destruction by fire which is total in nature. This is metaphorically spelled out in Jeremiah 11:16 where Israel is identified with a thriving olive tree with beautiful fruit which is struck down by a great storm with the result that its branches are broken. And it specifically mentions that God will set the tree on fire.

Thus, it is easy to see that the third (and final) block in Deuteronomy 29:22-29 (MT 29:21-28) and Jeremiah 11:9-17 are similar in the way that the two previous blocks in Deuteronomy 29 and in Jeremiah 11:1-17 correspond to each other. In other words, Deuteronomy 29 and Jeremiah 11:1-17 correspond structurally. Besides structural correspondence, Deuteronomy 29 and Jeremiah 11:1-17 share correspondence in language and content in terms of ideas.

We will examine now the similarities in language between Deuteronomy 29 and Jeremiah 11:1-17. The language relating to the covenant is similar in the two passages. The terms of the covenant,[10] or the requirement of the covenant,[11] are mentioned in both passages by the Hebrew – דִּבְרֵי הַבְּרִית (Deuteronomy 29:1, 9 [MT 28:69; 29:8] and Jeremiah 11:2, 3, 6, 8[12]). However, the similarity in specific language seems to stop there.[13] In fact, it is the difference in the

---

[10] Robert P. Carroll translates דִּבְרֵי הַבְּרִית as "the words of this covenant" (*Jeremiah: A Commentary* <London: SCM Press Ltd, 1986>, p. 266). William L. Holladay translates in the same way (*Jeremiah 1: A Commentary on the Book of the Prophet Jeremiah Chapters 1-25* <Philadelphia: Fortress Press, 1986>, pp. 346-347).

[11] Mackay, p. 396.

[12] דִּבְרֵי הַבְּרִית in Jeremiah 11:8 corresponds to the "curses of the covenant" – אָלוֹת הַבְּרִית – in Deuteronomy 29:21 (MT 29:20).

[13] Holladey writes regarding Jeremiah 11: "It is not enough to say that this material contains 'Deuteronomistic' phraseology. Verses 3-5 do, as will be shown, but for a specific reason; vv 6-14 do not..." (p. 350). The fact that Holladay qualifies even 'Deuteronomistic' portion with his words, "for a specific reason," is telling. Arguing for a strong Deuteronomistic influence in language seems to be a stretch.

language relating to the covenant in the two passages that highlights the distinctive quality of the Deuteronomy passage and of the Jeremiah passage.[14]

The language of the covenant indicates that Jeremiah was interested in emphasizing the obligation of Israelites to God and the failure of their obligation. This is clearly brought out in the language concerning the covenant. The Jeremiah emphasis on covenant-command is highlighted when we look at the language relating to the covenant in Deuteronomy. Deuteronomy 29 describes "making the covenant" or "cutting the covenant"–הַבְּרִית אֲשֶׁר־כָּרַת אִתָּם (Deuteronomy 29:1 [MT 28:69]). Deuteronomy 29:14 (MT 29:13) also uses the same language (כֹּרֵת אֶת־הַבְּרִית) with the idiomatic participle (אִתְּכֶם). Basically the same covenantal language is operating in Deuteronoy 29:25 (MT 29:24); that is, אֶת־בְּרִית יְהוָה אֱלֹהֵי אֲבֹתָם אֲשֶׁר כָּרַת עִמָּם and we note that עִמָּם is equivalent to אִתָּם coming from the same Hebrew word for "with" (עִם). Thus, we see that Deuteronomy uses the traditional formula and the idiomatic expression of making the covenant that expresses a two party participation in the process: God "cuts" a covenant "with" Israelites.

However, the Hebrew language expression is quite different in Jeremiah 11:1-17. The Jeremiah passage emphasizes that God commanded the covenant. Before focusing on the difference, it is important to note that there is one occurrence of the language of "cutting the covenant" in Jeremiah 11:1-17: אֶת־בְּרִיתִי אֲשֶׁר כָּרַתִּי אֶת־אֲבוֹתָם (verse 10). This shows that Jeremiah 11:1-17 block is aware of the traditional language in describing the making of the covenant with God. In fact, it is the presence of this classic formula that highlights the difference found in Jeremiah 11:1-17. Instead of repeating the formula as Deuteronomy 29 does in expressing God's making of the covenant with Israelites, Jeremiah 11:1-17 prefers the formula of God commanding the observance of the covenant. This is highlighted in the prologue to the block in Jeremiah. Whereas the prologue in Deuteronomy 29:1 (MT 28:69) uses the term "cut the covenant" two times, both in expressing the current making of the covenant and the past reality of the covenant made, Jeremiah 11:1-17 avoids using the phrase in its prologue found in Jeremiah 11. Instead, Jeremiah 11:2 focuses on the public proclamation of the covenant to the king and the people (שִׁמְעוּ אֶת־דִּבְרֵי הַבְּרִית הַזֹּאת וְדִבַּרְתָּם אֶל־אִישׁ יְהוּדָה וְעַל־יֹשְׁבֵי יְרוּשָׁלָםִ) and we see that God commands Jeremiah to hear the covenant and proclaim it to the "man of Judah" and the inhabitants of Jerusalem. There is nothing added after the phrase, אֶת־דִּבְרֵי הַבְּרִית הַזֹּאת, such as "which I made (כָּרַתִּי) with your fathers." Furthermore, there is no mention of God making a covenant with the Israelites of Jeremiah's day (*contra* Deuteronomy 29:1 [MT 28:69]).

---

[14] Jeremiah Unterman believes that Jeremiah has a fundamental difference with the literature and ideology of Deuteronomy and Kings (*From Repentance to Redemption: Jeremiah's Thought in Transition* <Sheffield: Sheffield Academic Press, 1987>, p. 21).

Jeremiah 11:2 indicates that the covenant הַבְּרִית (and דִּבְרֵי הַבְּרִית) functions like prophecy in Jeremiah 11:1-17. Just like in prophecy, where the word of God comes to the prophet who is to relay the prophetic words to the people, Jeremiah is to hear the covenant and relay it to the king and Jerusalem inhabitants. The language of covenant making or covenant renewal is missing. There is emphasis on the proclamation of the covenant.

The emphasis on the proclamation of the covenant continues in the language of Jeremiah that reiterates that God commands the covenant. Jeremiah 11:4 points out אֲשֶׁר צִוִּיתִי אֶת־אֲבוֹתֵיכֶם and we notice that אֲשֶׁר refers, in context, to אֶת־דִּבְרֵי הַבְּרִית הַזֹּאת found in verse 3. It is important to emphasize that "cut the covenant" language is not used here either; rather, "commanded the covenant" language is used. This Jeremiah language stands in contrast to the language in Deuteronomy. In Deuteronomy 29, the emphasis is on the covenant made between God and Israelites (or with the forefathers). In Jeremiah 11:1-17, the focus is on God's commanding the covenant to the forefathers and to the Israelites and requiring them to obey them.

The language of requiring obedience to the covenant is plentiful in Jeremiah 11:1-17. Jeremiah 11:6 further illustrates this point. God commands Jeremiah to "proclaim all of these words" (קְרָא אֶת־כָּל־הַדְּבָרִים הָאֵלֶּה). This prophetic-type proclamation is to be given in the cities of Judah and in the streets of Jerusalem. What is to be proclaimed? The inhabitants of Judah are to hear (שִׁמְעוּ) the covenant (אֶת־דִּבְרֵי הַבְּרִית הַזֹּאת) and do them (וַעֲשִׂיתֶם אוֹתָם).[15] The emphasis here is in the actual observance or practice of covenant obligations. Looking at Deuteronomy 29, we see that when God requires keeping of the covenant, the word used is not action-oriented or obedience-oriented like in Jeremiah. Rather, the Hebrew word for "keep" or "watch over" is used. This is best illustrated in Deuteronomy 29:9 (MT 29:8), וּשְׁמַרְתֶּם אֶת־דִּבְרֵי הַבְּרִית הַזֹּאת, which does not have the same focus on the action of doing as the verb here focuses on "watching over" or "guarding" the covenant.

In contrast to Deuteronomy, the explicit linguistic focus on obedience (in terms of action) to the covenant is overarching in Jeremiah 11:1-17. In Jeremiah 11:3, God commands Jeremiah to proclaim punishment to all those who do not even hear (לֹא יִשְׁמַע) the covenant (אֶת־דִּבְרֵי הַבְּרִית הַזֹּאת). The emphasis that all who hear (שִׁמְעוּ) must do them (וַעֲשִׂיתֶם אוֹתָם) is made in Jeremiah 11:4. "Hear and do" requirement for the covenant found in Jeremiah 11:3-4 is similar to the language of Jeremiah 11:6, discussed above.

The emphasis of the language of Jeremiah 11:1-17 on actively doing the requirements of the covenant in action is highlighted even in the Jeremiah language regarding the breaking of the covenant. Jeremiah 11:10 accuses Israelites (בֵּית־יִשְׂרָאֵל) and Judaeans (וּבֵית יְהוּדָה) of breaking (הֵפֵרוּ) the covenant

---

[15] Mackay argues that šama' ("to hear") points to the Hebrew idiom of šama baqôl ("to listen to the voice of" – verses 4 and 7), which has the sense of "to obey" (p. 397).

(אֶת־בְּרִיתִי). The verb "break" (הֵפֵרוּ) implies actual destruction of the covenant whereby the covenant is no longer in effect. In other words, a type of negative action against the covenant itself is seen to have been committed by Israelites and Judaeans. The language is quite different in Deuteronomy 29; unlike Jeremiah 11:10, it is not one of actual assault on the covenant. Rather, Deuteronomy 29:25 (MT 29:24) accuses Israelites of leaving (עָזְבוּ) the covenant (אֶת־בְּרִית יְהוָה). The verb employed in Deuteronomy 29:25 (MT 29:24) to indicate violation of the covenant is עָזְבוּ and means "leave" or "abandon"; thus, the verb indicates that the covenant could still be intact. No direct assault on the covenant has been committed and the covenant does not appear to be destroyed. The verb employed in Jeremiah 11:10 (הֵפֵרוּ) has a completely different denotation; it actually means that the covenant itself has been destroyed and not merely left behind possibly intact.

The finality of the broken covenant is highlighted in Jeremiah 11:1-17. The inevitability of God's destructive punishment[16] is pointed out in Jeremiah 11:11. God is bringing disaster (הִנְנִי מֵבִיא אֲלֵיהֶם רָעָה אֲשֶׁר לֹא־יוּכְלוּ לָצֵאת מִמֶּנָּה).[17] What is far worse than the fact that the disaster will be permanent is the second part of Jeremiah 11:11, where God states that he will refuse to listen[18] to penitent cries for divine help (וְזָעֲקוּ אֵלַי וְלֹא אֶשְׁמַע אֲלֵיהֶם). The idea that God will not listen to the prayers of Israelites when they cry out in their time of destruction is reiterated in Jeremiah 11:14 (אֵינֶנִּי שֹׁמֵעַ בְּעֵת קָרְאָם אֵלַי בְּעַד רָעָתָם).[19] The finality of the tragic punishment whereby God will not even listen to the prayers of Israelites is related to the fact that the covenant is destroyed.

The explicit finality of the response of God in Jeremiah 11:1-17 stands in contrast to Deuteronomy 29. It is true that Deuteronomy 29 also describes a horrible destruction. In fact, Deuteronomy 29 is more graphic in its description of total destruction (Deuteronomy 29:22-28 [MT 29:21-27]). God's punishment will include divine assault on the land (מַכּוֹת הָאָרֶץ הַהִוא – verse 22 [MT 21]), divine spreading of diseases in the land (תַּחֲלֻאֶיהָ אֲשֶׁר־חִלָּה יְהוָה בָּהּ, verse 22 [MT 21]), explosive and chemical wiping out of all the land (גָּפְרִית וָמֶלַח שְׂרֵפָה כָל־אַרְצָהּ,

---

[16] Holladay writes: "There was a chance to be saved, earlier, when Yahweh's warnings came in Josiah's generation, but the people have lost it by reverting to the way they have been pursuing before Josiah's time" (p. 356).

[17] Regarding הִנְנִי מֵבִיא אֲלֵיהֶם רָעָה, Holladay states that it is not found in Deuteronomy at all and comments further: "Nothing like it is there" (p. 351).

[18] Thomas W. Overholt states that a false sense of security stopped the Judaeans (Israelites) from responding to God's demand for repentance and this was one of the threats of falsehood that faced them (*The Threat of Falsehood: A Study in the Theology of the book of Jeremiah* <Naperville: Alec R. Allenson Inc., 1970>, p. 1).

[19] Louis Stulman sees the portions in Jeremiah 11:11, 14 referring to the fact that God will not listen to the prayers as being the same in the Masoretic Text and the Old Greek (LXXV) (*The Other Text of Jeremiah: A Reconstruction of the Hebrew Text Underlying the Greek Version of the Prose Sections of Jeremiah wth English Translation* <Lanham: University Press of America, 1985>, p. 27).

verse 23 [MT 22]), including all vegetation. Despite the fact that the destruction is described in Deuteronomy 29 to be complete and all-encompassing, there is not a single explicit sentence to state that God will not listen to any prayers. The implication is that although God is punishing Israelites for abandoning the covenant, the covenant may still be intact and God will hear prayers on account of the still intact covenant.[20] However, Jeremiah 11:1-17 concludes that the covenant is broken, so there is no more covenant that is intact. Thus, God will ignore and not listen to any prayers because the covenantal relationship is severed and, more importantly, there is no longer a covenant in effect.[21] And Jeremiah is forbidden to pray for their salvation.[22]

The language of Jeremiah shows that Jeremiah 11:1-17 was interested in emphasizing the obligation of Israelites to obey the covenant and their failure in this regard. Furthermore, Jeremiah's language indicates the concern to emphasize that the covenant is broken and no longer in effect. The language of Jeremiah 11:1-17 is different from that of Deuteronomy 29. A question rises: Why is there such a difference in language and emphasis?

I would argue that the difference highlights the difference of genre.[23] Deuteronomy 29 is a record-keeping historical document meant to focus on the continuity rather than the discontinuity. However, Jeremiah 11:1-17[24] is a prophetic, oracular[25] document[26] that is meant to focus on the discontinuity,

---

[20] It must be noted that the idea of the finality of destruction for covenant breaking is present in Jeremiah 29 as well. In Deuteronomy 29:20 (MT 29:19), God says that he will not forgive (לֹא־יֹאבֶה יְהוָה סְלֹחַ). One can argue that God's not willing to forgive covenant-breakers is akin to his not hearing their prayers.

[21] Mackay recognizes that during God's judgment, Israelites will recognize their wrongdoing, but that realization will be too late and useless; God will not listen to them (p. 402).

[22] Cf. Jeremiah 7:16; 14:11; 15:1. Carolyn J. Sharp describes this prohibition of Jeremiah's prayer on behalf of Israelites/Judahites as "the culminating blow in proclamations of judgement" (*Prophecy and Ideology in Jeremiah: Struggles for Authority in the Deutero-Jeremianic Prose* <London: T. & T. Clark, 2003>, p. 47).

[23] Some scholars believe that Jeremiah opposed Deuteronomy way of thinking (Henri Cazelles, "Jeremiah and Deuteronomy," trans. Leo G. Perdue, *A Prophet to the Nations: Essays in Jeremiah Studies*, ed. Leo G. Perdue and Brian W. Kovacs <Winona Lake: Eisenbrauns, 1984, pp. 89-111>, pp. 92, 98-101).

[24] Mowinckel identified Jeremiah 11:1-14 as source C (Siegfried Herrmann, *Jeremia: Der Prophet und das Buch* <Darmstadt: Wissenschaftliche Buchgesellschaft, 1990>, p. 59).

[25] In *From Chaos to Covenant*, Carroll states: "The primary datum about Isaiah, Jeremiah, Ezekiel, Amos or any of the biblical prophets is that they were poets" (p. 11), and Carroll uses the term "oracles" (p. 60) and "prophetic poetry" (p. 61) to describe Jeremiah. Cazelle also identifies Jeremiah's writing as "oracles" (p. 97).

[26] Taro Odashima refers to Jeremiah as "Jermia-Archiv" (*Heilsworte im Jeremiabuch: Untersuchungen zu ihrer vordeuteronomistischen Bearbeitung* <Stuttgart: Verlag W. Kohlhammer, 1989>, p. 1).

rather than the continuity. While being different in this way, both Deuteronomy 29 and Jeremiah 11:1-17 share a commonality; that is, they are both interested in exonerating God from any blame for the total destruction of Israel and death of Israelites.[27] Thus, both of them can be seen as written in defense of God and to point out the culpability of the Israelites. Indeed, it is possible to say that the overarching theme of both Deuteronomy 29 and Jeremiah 11:1-17 is the same. However, it is important to note their differences in focus, especially in regards to the covenant. Even though they both want to defend God and his actions in completely destroying Israel and killing Israelites in the process, Deuteronomy 29 focuses on the continuity after the destruction, and Jeremiah 11:1-19 focuses on the discontinuity. We will see how this is achieved.

First, let us examine Deuteronomy 29. Deuteronomy 29 is a record-keeping historical document that focuses on the continuity. It is possible to say that history by nature focuses on the continuity. The reason for this is clear. History is writing by later generations to see the cause and effect of history. But fundamentally, history is written by a people to remember their past and its continuity to the present. Thus, it may be possible to generalize and say that all historical writing as principle connects the past with the present and looks at events as continuous.

The concern with record and detail is a part of this historical concern with the connection to the past. The prologue to the document highlights its historical nature. Deuteronomy 29:1 (MT 28:69) adds extraneous detail of historical nature, מִלְּבַד הַבְּרִית אֲשֶׁר־כָּרַת אִתָּם בְּחֹרֵב ("in addition to the covenant which he cut with them in Horeb").[28] This detail is not necessary but is added because of the genre of the text, which is a record-keeping historical document. In fact, the whole of Deuteronomy 29:2-8 (MT 29:1-7) can be seen as a record-keeping detail of a historian. Furthermore, Deuteronomy 29:10-11 (MT 29:9-10) highlights the historical genre of the text by listing all those who are gathered in detail. The list describes Gentiles living with the Israelites (וְגֵרְךָ אֲשֶׁר בְּקֶרֶב מַחֲנֶיךָ). And we even find out what these Gentiles do – they chop the wood of Israelites and carry their water (מֵחֹטֵב עֵצֶיךָ עַד שֹׁאֵב מֵימֶיךָ). These are details with which a record-keeping historian would be concerned.

---

[27] Carroll notes that Jeremiah 11:1-17 represented an attempt to defend God since the destruction of the community in 587 could have been seen as God's inability to protect them (*Jeremiah: A Commentary*, p. 270).

[28] This contrasts with the covenant mentioned in Jeremiah 11:1-17. Walter Brueggemann writes regarding Jeremiah 11:1-5 that there "is no hint of what covenant" (*To Pluck Up, To Tear Down: A Commentary on the Book of Jeremiah 1-25* <Grand Rapids: Wm. B. Eerdmans Publishing Co., 1988>, p. 104). Brueggemann adds that following verses show what covenant is being referred to–that of the Sinaitic covenant. Brueggeman adds that the Sinaitic covenant stood in confrontation to the royal covenant valued by the Jerusalem elite.

And like a historian, there is a concern with continuity. Deuteronomy 29:22-24 (MT 29:21-23) is particularly insightful in this regard. This passage recognizes the potential of a total destruction of Israel by God in divine judgment. However, it identifies three groups of people who may see the result of the divine destruction who may ask questions regarding it (in the aftermath); they are the surviving descendants of the Israelites who had been destroyed because they broke the covenant (הַדּוֹר הָאַחֲרוֹן בְּנֵיכֶם אֲשֶׁר יָקוּמוּ מֵאַחֲרֵיכֶם), foreigners who see the devastation (וְהַנָּכְרִי אֲשֶׁר יָבֹא מֵאֶרֶץ רְחוֹקָה וְרָאוּ), and all the nations (כָּל־הַגּוֹיִם). The very concern with the past is historical in nature. Deuteronomy 29 emphasizes the historical nature of its text by having people of the "future" raise questions about the past. For the historian, continuity in history or in historical questioning is important regardless of cataclysmic or apocalyptic events. Things are different for prophetic literature.

Jeremiah 11:1-17 shows itself to be prophetic, oracular literature in terms of genre.[29] It contrasts with Deuteronomy 29 in that there is not a historian's concern with continuity after complete destruction.[30] The focus in Jeremiah 11:1-7 is on the destruction itself and the finality of that destruction. We have seen how the language of Jeremiah 11:1-17 expresses the finality of the cataclysmic judgment. The covenant is broken, and, therefore, it no longer exists. Thus, God will not listen to suffering and dying people who are experiencing divine judgement and retribution even when they pray in earnestness. There is

---

[29] It is possible to say that designating any text as "prophetic" or "oracular" emphasizes the reality that it was delivered in that tradition, as H. Lalleman-de Winkel writes that "prophecy was relevant at a certain moment in a certain period of Israel's history" (*Jeremiah in Prophetic Tradition: An Examination of the Book of Jeremiah in the Light of Israel's Prophetic Traditions* <Leuven: Peeters, 2000>, p. 15). However, it is important to note that due to the fact that prophetic oracles of Jeremiah went from oral form to written form, it is important to recognize the concern for audience that undergirded the process from orality to written text (See Louis Stulman, *Order Amid Chaos: Jeremiah as Symbolic Tapestry* <Sheffield: Sheffield Academic Press, 1998>). What this means is that the content of prophecy was seen as applicable in the present and the future of the community for which the fulfilled oracles of the past were written down. It can be said also that communities that receive Jeremiah and retain it in their religious worship and communal reading necessarily take the prophecy as applying to them. Thus, Jeremiah would be read as having been fulfilled in the destruction of Jerusalem in 70 AD by those who maintained the reading of that text at that time. Thus, one can speak about the Sitz im Leben of the oracle, the Sitz im Buch of the oracle, and the Sitz im Lesung of the oracle.

[30] Claus Westermann argues that pre-exilic prophets were prophets of doom. In other words, pre-exilic prophets were, like Jeremiah 11:1-17, emphasizing that there was no hope for salvation once God's judgement was on the way. In fact, for Westermann prophecy of doom was true prophecy, and calls for repentance was post-exilic redaction and not prophetic in nature (*Grundformen prophetischen Rede* <München: Kaiser, 1971>, pp. 130-149). W. Thiel agrees (*Die deuteronomistische Redaktion von Jeremia 1-25* <Neukirchen-Vluyn: Neukirchener Verlag, 1981>, p. 290).

no indication, either explicit or implicit, in Jeremiah 11:1-17 that there is a future after this complete judgement by God. The implication is that the end judgment will come and that will be all. In the context of Jeremiah 11:1-17, there is not even a mention of a surviving remnant. The focus is on the utter destruction in prophetic doom. In this regard, Jeremiah 11:1-17 testifies for itself the identity of a pure prophetic, oracular text.

The prophetic, oracular genre nature of Jeremiah 11:1-17 is highlighted in the introduction and the conclusion of the prophetic doom. In the beginning, there is a prophetic curse formula, אָרוּר הָאִישׁ לֹא יִשְׁמַע אֶת־דִּבְרֵי הַבְּרִית הַזֹּאת ("Let the one who does not listen to the words of the covenant be damned!" – Jeremiah 11:2). This oracular–or prophetic doom–formula marks Jeremiah 11:1-17 as a prophetic, or oracular, document. Likewise, the conclusion of Jeremiah 11:1-17 indicates its genre as a prophetic, oracular document. Jeremiah 11:1-17 concludes the prophetic oracle of doom by stating the curse formula; that is, וַיהוָה צְבָאוֹת הַנּוֹטֵעַ אוֹתָךְ דִּבֶּר עָלַיִךְ רָעָה ("And the LORD of Heavenly Armies who established you has decreed evil against you!"–Jeremiah 11:17).

It is interesting to see the connection between Deuteronomy 29 and Jeremiah 11:1-17. There are similarities in structure–the corresponding analogous two blocks plus one conclusion block–that seem to indicate some form of commonality between the two texts. There is also similarity in language and ideas between Deuteronomy 29 and Jeremiah 11:1-17. This may be due to the fact that both of the texts describe the covenant with God, its obligations, and its curses for violation. However, it is the difference between Deuteronomy 29 and Jeremiah 11:1-17 that points to the nature of the relationship between the texts.

I would conclude that Jeremiah 11:1-17 is dependent on Deuteronomy because it is Jeremiah 11:1-17 that deviates from the classic language of covenant-making. This was done, of course, for the purpose of focus on God's demand for obedience to the covenant. Furthermore, it is Jeremiah 11:1-17's genre–that of prophetic, oracular document–which provided the forum for such a difference in language and idea emphasis.

However, it is important to understand that despite the difference in language and emphasis in ideas, both Deuteronomy 29 and Jeremiah 11:1-17 agree on the central principles: God completely destroys covenant breakers and their nation and kills its inhabitants. And there is a point at which God will not forgive those who repent because the judgement of God has begun against covenant breakers and God's divine wrath will be satisfied through the successful completion of the divine destruction, killing, and judgment.

Bibliography

Buber, Martin. *The Prophetic Persona: Jeremiah and the Language of the Self.* Sheffield: JSOT Press, 1984.

Brueggemann, Walter. *To Pluck Up, To Tear Down: A Commentary on the Book of Jeremiah 1-25.* Grand Rapids: Wm. B. Eerdmans Publishing Co., 1988.

Carroll, Robert P. *From Chaos to Covenant: Uses of Prophecy in the Book of Jeremiah.* London: SCM Press Ltd, 1981.

Carroll, Robert P. *Jeremiah: A Commentary.* London: SCM Press Ltd, 1986.

Diamond, A. R. Pete, Kathleen M. O'Connor, and Louis Stulman (Editors). *Troubling Jeremiah.* Sheffield: Sheffield Academic Press, 1999.

Friebel, Kelvin G. *Jeremiah's and Ezekiel's Sign-Acts.* Sheffield: Sheffield Academic Press, 1999.

Goldman, Yohanan. *Prophétie et royauté au retour de l'exil: Les origins littéraires de la forme massorétique du livre de Jérémie.* Freiburg: Universitätsverlag, 1992.

Groß, Walter (Editor). *Jeremia und die »deuteronomistische Bewegung«.* Weinheim: Beltz Athenäum Verlag, 1995.

Herrmann, Siegfried. *Jeremia: Der Prophet und das Buch.* Darmstadt: Wissenschaftliche Buchgesellschaft, 1990.

Holladay, William L. *Jeremiah 1: A Commentary on the Book of the Prophet Jeremiah Chapters 1-25.* Philadelphia: Fortress Press, 1986.

King, Philip J. *Jeremiah: An Archaeological Campanion.* Louisville: Westminster/John Knox Press, 1993.

Laato, Antti. *History and Ideology in the Old Testament Prophetic Literature: A Semiotic Approach to the Reconstruction of the Proclamation of the Historical Prophets.* Stockholm: Almqwist & Wiksell International, 1996.

Lalleman-de Winkel, H. *Jeremiah in Prophetic Tradition: An Examination of the Book of Jeremiah in the Light of Israel's Prophetic Traditions.* Leuven: Peeters, 2000.

Mackay, John L. *Jeremiah: An Introduction and Commentary (Volume 1: Chapters 1-20).* Fearn: Mentor, 2004.

Nicholson, E. W. *Preaching to the Exiles: A Study of the Prose Tradition in the Book of Jeremiah.* Oxford: Basil Blackwell, 1970.

Odashima, Taro. *Heilsworte im Jeremiabuch: Untersuchungen zu ihrer vordeuteronomistischen Bearbeitung.* Stuttgart: Verlag W. Kohlhammer, 1989.

Overholt, Thomas W. *The Threat of Falsehood: A Study in the Theology of the Book of Jeremiah.* Naperville: Alec R. Allenson Inc., 1970.

Perdue, Leo G., and Brian W. Kovacs (Editors). *A Prophet to the Nations: Essay in Jeremiah Studies.* Winona Lake: Eisenbrauns, 1984.

Polk, Timothy. *The Prophetic Persona: Jeremiah and the Language of the Self.* Sheffield: JSOT Press, 1984.

Roncace, Mark. *Jeremiah, Zedekiah, and the Fall of Jerusalem.* New York: T. & T. Clark, 2005.

Sharp, Carolyn J. *Prophecy and Ideology in Jeremiah: Struggle for Authority in the Deutero-Jeremianic Prose.* London: T. & T. Clark, 2003.

Stulman, Louis. *Order Amid Chaos: Jeremiah as Symbolic Tapestry.* Sheffield: Sheffield Academic Press, 1998.

Stulman, Louis. *The Other Text of Jeremiah: A Reconstruction of the Hebrew Text Underlying the Greek Version of the Prose Sections of Jeremiah with English Translation.* Lanham: University Press of America, 1985.

Sweeney, Marvin A. *King Josiah of Judah: The Lost Messiah of Israel.* New York: Oxford University Press, 2001.

Thiel, W. *Die deuteronomistische Redaaktion von Jeremia 1-25.* Neukirchen-Vluyn: Neukirchener Verlag, 1973.

Unterman, Jeremiah. *From Repentance to Redemption: Jeremiah's Thought in Transition.* Sheffield: Sheffield Academic Press, 1987.

Weiser, Artur. *Das Buch Jeremia.* Göttingen: Vandenhoek & Ruprecht, 1969.

Westermann, Claus. *Grundformen prophetischer Rede.* München: Kaiser, 1971.

"Luke 4:14-30 and Its Socio-Historical Context of Galilee For Understanding Jesus of Nazareth and the Jesus Movement"[1]

Jesus' Nazareth Sermon (Luke 4:14-30) provides significant information regarding the nature of early Jesus movement and is a key to understanding the development of Christianity that spread beyond Palestine. Most significant in this Lukan pericope is the quote of Isaiah 61:1-2[2] found in Luke 4:18-19 and the way Jesus of Nazareth interprets this passage. Jesus of Nazareth explains the fulfilment in terms of Gentile mission in Luke 4:25-27. The iconoclast nature of Jesus' sermons is, in fact, congruent with the picture of Jesus movement in the socio-historical[3] context of Galilee. In this paper, we will examine the nature of religiosity in Galilee and how Jesus movement fits into this context. Then, we will examine specifically the nature of Jesus' sermon and its implications for the study of early Christianity.

Galilee during Jesus' time was seen as rife with popular religiosity. Some scholars have pointed to the stories of Hanina ben Dosa as an example of the kind of popular religiosity that was a bit eccentric. Rabbinic documents describe Hanina ben Dosa as a first century AD rabbi who performed miracles and lived

---

[1] This article is based on my academic paper presented at the Scripture in Early Judaism and Christianity Section of the 2006 Annual Meeting of the Society of Biblical Literature in Washington, D.C.

[2] Luke 4:18-19 contains the New Testament's only citation of Isaiah 61:1-2 (with Isaiah 58:6) (Charles A. Kimball, *Jesus' Exposition of the Old Testament in Luke's Gospel* [Sheffield: Sheffield Academic Press, 1994], p. 97). See also Traught Holtz, *Untersuchungen über die alttestamentlichen Zitate bei Lukas* (Berlin: Akademie Verlag, 1968), p. 40.

[3] Abraham J. Malherbe writes: "The sociological approach to early Christianity is to be welcomed as one method among others that we may utilize. That a clearer view of Christian communities will help us to understand both early Christianity and its literature better is surely beyond doubt" (*Social Aspects of Early Christianity* <Baton Rouge: Louisiana State University, 1997>, p. 11).

in total poverty. Hanina ben Dosa was born around 20 AD in Sepphoris, ten miles north of Nazareth. He was identified with the prophet Elijah.[4] The fact that Jerusalem was far from Nazareth and Galilee could have had something to do with the presence of popular mystic-types. Whereas Jerusalem and its immediate surroundings were within the purview of control by official leaders of the Jerusalem cult, Galilee was too far away to be adequately controlled by Jerusalem leaders. Certainly, difficulty of travel had something to contribute to the lack of tight control on the recess regions of Israel. But there were other factors as well. Galilee was separated from Jerusalem by Samaria, and given the Jewish perception of Samaritans, it is understandable why many religious Jews of Jerusalem may have been reluctant to travel frequently through or near Samaria into Galilee. Furthermore, Israelite society during the time of Jesus of Nazareth was parochial. Thus, Judaeans were not necessarily interested in fraternizing with Galileans[5] and vice versa. Regionalism provided independence for Galileans, which popular charismatics were eager to exploit. In fact, because Jerusalem was tightly controlled by Jerusalem Temple cult leadership, while Galilee was not, Jesus was able to carry out his ministry in Galilee[6] without a systematic process to his execution by Jewish authorities,[7] localized primarily in

---

[4] Michael Grant, *Jesus: An Historian's Review of the Gospels* (New York: Charles Scribner's Sons, 1977), pp. 33, 69.

[5] It is interesting to note that there are a series of five controversies between Jesus of Nazareth and the Pharisees in Galilee which escalate Pharisaic hostility to Jesus of Nazareth. However, the Pharisees seem missing when Jesus of Nazareth enters Jerusalem (David B. Gowler, *Host, Guest, Enemy and Friend: Portraits of the Pharisees in Luke and Acts* <New York: Peter Lang, 1991>, pp. 298-299). Michael Bachmann writes: "Zwar warden die Pharisäer bei Lukas, in dessen Werk diese Gruppe anders als bei Matthhäus und Markus deutlich als im Synedrium vertreten gekennzeichnet wird, -- jedenfalls in kollektiver Weise – nirgends explizit zum Tempel in Beziehung gesetzt..." (*Jerusalem und der Tempel: Die geographisch-theologischen Elemente in der lukanischen Sicht des jüdischen Kultzentrums* <Stuttgart: Verlag W. Kohlhammer, 1980>, p. 201). This raises the question of the marginality of the Pharisaic movement within Jerusalem Jewish leadership or the dominance of the Temple cult and its priestly tradition in Jerusalem (over the Pharisees).

[6] Jesus of Nazareth's disciples was later designated "Galileans," or those who came up to Jerusalem with Jesus from Galilee (Hans Conzelmann, *The Theology of St. Luke*, trans. Geoffrey Buswell <Philadelphia: Fortress Press, 1982>, p. 38).

[7] David L. Tiede notes that the very moment Jesus of Nazareth entered Jerusalem, the Jerusalem Jewish religious establishment organized an opposition and put process in motion to get Jesus of Nazareth killed (*Prophecy and History in Luke-Acts* [Philadelphia: Fortress Press, 1980], p. 105). Jack Dean Kingsbury states: "In Luke, as in Mark and Matthew, the matter of 'authority' lies at the heart of the conflict between Jesus and the religious authorities" (*Conflict in Luke: Jesus, Authorities, Disciples* <Minneapolis: Fortress Press, 1991>, p. 81).

Jerusalem.[8] Morton Scott Enslin states that "Jesus' first visit to Jerusalem [was] his last."[9] David Flusser writes: "He wanted to die in Jerusalem, reputed for 'killing the prophets and stoning those who are sent to you' (Lk. 13:34)."[10]

In this religious atmosphere, Jesus of Nazareth fits into the mold of wandering charismatics.[11] Günther Bornkamm denies the possibility of Jesus of Nazareth being a rabbi[12] based on this fact: "Also in his daily life, we have seen, Jesus moves about with an informality which does not fit the picture and customs of a rabbi, at least as we know them from later texts: among his followers are women; children are allowed to approach him; he sits down at table with tax collectors, sinners, and prostitutes (Lk. Vii. 39)."[13] However, what separated Jesus of Nazareth from other wandering charismatics was that Jesus of Nazareth tended to be radical in his teachings even by Galilean standards. Heidelberg University's Professor Gerd Theissen's reconstruction of Jesus of Nazareth's ministry in his book, *The Shadow of the Galilean: The Quest of the Historical Jesus in Narrative Form*, is insightful. Written as a narrative reconstruction with the fictional character of Andreas thrown in, the account is entertaining as well. But Theissen emphasizes the historical accuracy of the description of the ancient society: "In essence, I am concerned to do only one thing: to sketch in narrative form a picture of Jesus and his time which both does justice to the present state of scholarly research and is understandable to

---

[8] Floyd V. Filson states that Jesus of Nazareth's "final visit to Jerusalem, where concentrated opposition was sure to be met" indicated that he was not quick to leave Galilee, where he enjoyed relative safety (*A New Testament History: The Story of the Emerging Church* <Philadelphia: The Westminster Press, 1964>, p. 107).

[9] Morton Scott Enslin, *The Prophet from Nazareth* (New York: McGraw-Hill Book Company, Inc., 1961), p. 41.

[10] David Flusser, *Jesus*, trans. Ronald Walls (New York: Herder and Herder, 1969), p. 105.

[11] Gerd Theissen notes that Jesus of Nazareth set the example of a wandering charismatic and expected it in his disciples. Theissen writes: "Homelessness belonged to the discipleship of Jesus, and not merely during his lifetime. The *Didache*, for example, is familiar with itinerant Christian charistmatics and says that they practice πρόπους κυρίου, the Lord's way of living (*Did.* 11.8)" (*Social Reality and the Early Christians: Theology, Ethics, and the World of the New Testament*, trans. Margaret Kohl <Minneapolis: Fortress Press, 1992>, pp. 37-38). In Matthew 8:20, Jesus of Nazareth says: "Foxes have holes and birds of the air have nests, but the Son of Man has no place to lay his head."

[12] Wayne A. Meeks actually does not like the term 'rabbi' being applied to pre-second century AD settings since the earliest 'rabbinic Judaism' documents were compiled at the end of the second century AD. Meeks writes: "We will do well to avoid using the term *rabbi* or *rabbinic* of any phenomenon earlier than the academy founded at Yavneh (Jamnia) by Yohanan ben Zakkai, and we will be on safer ground to restrict these terms to second-century and later developments" (*The First Urban Christians: The Social World of the Apostle Paul* <New Haven: Yale University Press, 1983>, p. 33).

[13] Günther Bornkamm, *Jesus of Nazareth*, trans. Irene and Fraser McLuskey with James M. Robinson (New York: Harper & Brothers Publishers, 1960), p. 97.

present-day readers."[14] Theissen describes negative Jewish perception of Jesus of Nazareth's radical teaching in the words of a character named Susanna: "Someone once came to his master wanting to follow him, but first he had to bury his dead father. Jesus said, 'Let the dead bury their dead' and told the man to follow him immediately. Isn't that inhuman? Aren't parents worth anything any more? Are we parents worth no more than animal corpses, that one need not bury?"[15] Jürgen Becker comments regarding Luke 9:59-60 (cf. Matthew 8:21-22): "The possibility that one would not honor one's parent in such a situation would not even have entered anyone's mind. Jesus' answer must have shocked and offended his hearers, therefore, when he said, *Let the dead bury their dead!*"[16] Although not as emphatic as Theissen in attributing Galilean setting as the cause for Jesus of Nazareth's eccentric position, Jürgen Becker agrees that Jesus' hostility to family set him apart from traditional Judaism. This is the case that is found in Luke 14:26 (cf. Matthew 10:37) as well, which more explicitly states that one has to hate one's parents to be a disciple of Jesus of Nazareth.[17] Becker describes this teaching of Jesus as indicative of a theological re-evaluation of family in light of Jesus of Nazareth's teaching on the Kingdom of God which he described as being realized in the present, at least in part.[18] For Jesus of Nazareth, loyalty to the Kingdom of God [19] took precedent over observing the Ten Commandments. Even though Becker emphasizes the theological dimension more than Theissen, he essentially agrees with Theissen in viewing the importance of the Galilean background. Becker writes: "Are the table-fellowships in Galilean villages, miracles, conflicts about the Sabbath, etc. not glimpses of the public activity of Jesus with a biographical interest?"[20]

So, what was Galilee like at the time of Jesus of Nazareth? Bornkamm describes it as "semi-pagan, despised Galilee."[21] James H. Snowden describes Galilee as "a provincial district" and "so obscure and despised a place."[22] John

---

[14] Gerd Theissen, *The Shadow of the Galilean: The Quest of the Historical Jesus in Narrative Form*, trans. John Bowden (London: SCM Press Ltd, 1987), p. 1.

[15] Theissen, *The Shadow of the Galilean*, p. 72.

[16] Jürgen Becker, *Jesus of Nazareth*, trans. James E. Crouch (New York:Walter de Gruyter, 1998), p. 115.

[17] Theissen notes that Jesus of Nazareth's demand for breaking with family relations for discipleship is tied to willingness to give up a fixed place of abode" (*Social Reality and the Early Christians*, p. 38).

[18] Becker, pp. 309-310.

[19] Bart D. Ehrman notes that Jesus' Kingdom of God pointed to an actual and literal kingdom with power on earth and not "in purely symbolic terms about God becoming the ruler of your heart" (*Jesus: Apocalyptic Prophet of the New Millennium* <New York: Oxford University Press, 1999>, p. 143).

[20] Becker, p. 21.

[21] Bornkamm, p. 53.

[22] Snowden, James H. *Jesus as Judged by His Enemies: A Study of the Criticisms and Attacks Made on Jesus by His Enemies* (New York: The Abingdon Press, 1922), p. 23.

Dominic Crossan takes the position that Lower Galilee was urbane as any other city in the Roman Empire.[23] Eduard Lohse, however, points to the reality that urbanity may have belonged to wealthy Gentile landowners in Galilee. Lohse writes: "Since large parts of the Galilean hill country were originally royal lands, even in the Hellenistic period many farms belonged to non-Jews who lived in other countries and managed their property through administrators. The Jewish population of the country earned their living by farming, handicraft, and small businesses."[24] In fact, Michael Grant notes:

> The Galileans have not been Jewish for long. Although there may have been a few Jews there at an earlier period, it was only under the Maccabee (Hasmonean) ruler of Judaea John Hyrcanus I, at the end of the second century BC, that the country had been attached to the main homeland and converted by official declaration to Judaism. But the conversion had never affected more than about half the population of Galilee, and at the time of Jesus it still contained numerous pagans. Moreover, those of its inhabitants who were Jews were not always regarded as 'sound', being frequently attacked by spiritual establishment in Judaea for religious ignorance and ritual impropriety and for dietic and other uncleanness.[25]

The picture of Galilee at the time of Jesus of Nazareth was one of instability and distance from the Jerusalem Temple cult in terms of distance and influence. It was in this environment that charismatic movements and leadership was able to thrive. Furthermore, it is important to note that Galilee was surrounded by Hellenistic areas dominated by non-Jews. Christoph Burchard describes: "Overall, Galilee was surrounded by Hellenistic city-states, which were self-governed within the province of Syria. Those to the southeast and east formed a loose federation, the Decapolis. Jews lived in all states as more or less strong minorities."[26] In terms of languages, there was a kind of confusion in Galilee. There were three languages–Hebrew, Aramaic, and Greek–in Galilee, but Albert Schweitzer notes that it is difficult to know which language was the primary and

---

[23] John Dominic Crossan, *The Historical Jesus: The Life of a Mediterranean Jewish Peasant* (San Francisco: HarperSanFrancisco, 1991), p. 19.
[24] Eduard Lohse, *The New Testament Environment*, trans. John E. Steely (Nashville: Abingdon, 1976), p. 147.
[25] Grant, p. 74.
[26] Christoph Burchard, "Jesus of Nazareth" in *Christian Beginnings: Word and Community from Jesus to Post-Apostolic Times*, ed. Jürgen Becker, trans. Annemarie S. Kidder and Reinhard Krauss (Louisville: Westminster/John Knox Press, 1993, pp. 15-72), p. 47.

which language was least spoken because "Josephus, the only writer who could have told us, fails us in this point, as he so often does elsewhere."[27]

Given the demographics and history of Galilee, it is not surprising why Jesus of Nazareth sermon was so offensive to Jews. It privileged Gentiles over Jews where Jewish place was not really secure. But besides the demographics, there is a deeper reason for the offence to Judaism. If we look at later Rabbinic writings on Gentiles, we can understand the extent of this offence. Rabbi Judah said that Jews should say three prayers: "Blessed be he who did not make me a Gentile. Blessed be he who did not make me a woman. Blessed be he who did not make me an uneducated person. 'All Gentiles are nothing before him'" (Tosephta Berakhoth 7:18). Not only did Jews have a disdain of Gentiles for religious reasons, Jews disliked Gentiles on political grounds. Gentiles had the ultimate authority over Palestine, although the Jewish Sanhedrin was allowed to exercise its power as the supreme Jewish authority in the land.[28] The supreme authority of the Romans was felt from time to time. For instance, Luke 13:1 describes how Pilate's soldiers attacked Galilean pilgrims in the Jerusalem Temple area and killed them, so that their blood mixed with their sacrifices. F. F. Bruce notes that it was more as the result of Pilate's dislike of the tetrarch of Galilee that he killed Galileans, rather than his dislike of the Galileans.[29] Whatever may have been the case, Pilate's willingness to kill Galilean Jews who entered his jurisdiction indiscriminately shows the uncertain place of Jews in Palestine. Such cases probably were not isolated or infrequent. Given the political circumstance, it would not be surprising to find radical hostility among Jews against Gentiles. Jesus of Nazareth's sermon of privileging Jews over Genitiles would have found hostility from this standpoint as well.

Furthermore, scriptural tradition, particularly those belonging close to the Second Temple period, seemed to be anti-Gentile. For instance, one of the strongest traditions is the hostility to intermarriage. In the book of Ezra, there is a demand for divorcing non-Jewish wives. Ezra 10:10-11 states: "Then Ezra the priest stood up and said to them, 'You have been unfaithful; you have married foreign women, adding to Israel's guilt. Now make confession to the LORD, the God of your fathers, and do his will. Separate yourselves from the peoples around you and from your foreign wives.'" This religious trend against intermarriage was not unique to the early Second Temple period. The force of this religious position is felt in the late Second Temple period and beyond.

In light of socio-historical condition of Galilee at the time of Jesus of Nazareth, Jesus of Nazareth's sermon in the Lukan pericope can be placed in the

---

[27] Albert Schweitzer, *The Quest of the Historical Jesus: A Critical Study of Its Progress from Reimarus to Wrede*, trans. W. Montgomery (New York: MacMillan Publishing Co., Inc., 1968), p. 274.
[28] Lohse, p. 147.
[29] F. F. Bruce, *New Testament History* (New York: Doubleday & Company, Inc., 1971), p. 37.

context of Jesus of Nazareth's time in Galilee. The pericope itself exhibits tensions that were found in Galilee, where Jews and Gentiles existed side-by-side. The angry reaction (Luke 4:28) of the Jewish crowd in the synagogue after Jesus of Nazareth's sermon found in Luke 4:24-27, privileging Gentiles over Jews, can be seen as normative in light of the tensions that existed at the time of Jesus of Nazareth between Jews and Gentiles in Galilee. Especially as the Jewish identity of the region was not secure, it can be understandable from a sociological standpoint how the crowd could flare up to mob violence with intent to kill Jesus of Nazareth by throwing him over the cliff (Luke 4:29). However, due to lack of solid central Jewish religious authority in the region as in Jerusalem, the potential violence remained mob violence rather than organized and systematic arrest and delivery of capital punishment.

The sermon of Luke 4:24-27 fits into the Sitz im Leben of Jesus of Nazareth. Before continuing on with proof in this regard, we will look at other possibilities in a critical way. Some scholars may date Luke 4:24-27 (and even the whole pericope) to a much later period.[30] They may claim the sermon as originating in the later Jewish versus Christian conflict after the fall of Jerusalem in 70 AD. It is true that there seem to be vivid conflicts in the Second Century AD between Jews and Christians as witnessed in the writings of Justin Martyr and other Church Fathers. However, I would argue that this pericope was originally composed certainly before the destruction of the Second Temple. First of all, the very fact that Justin Martyr and Church Fathers engage Jews and are concerned to engage Jews in Christian apologetics is significant.[31] In a sense, their writings can be seen not only as defending Christianity against those who oppose it, but also as an effort to convert those who oppose Christianity. Since many apologetic writings address Jews and Judaism, it is clear that there was interest in converting Jews. This does not fit into the sermon of Jesus of Nazareth found in Luke 4:24-27. Jesus of Nazareth tells of Elijah ignoring Jews and Elisha as ignoring Jews; they rather minister to Gentiles. The important factor to note here is the content of the message. Jesus of Nazareth's sermon in Luke 4:24-27 does not have as its purpose converting Jews; it is a proclamation not meant to be apologetic or proselytizing in any way. This was certainly not the case in writings of Church Fathers where there is an apologetic dialogue that inherently assumes the desire to convert Jews.

Second of all, this pericope originated before the destruction of the Jerusalem Temple because of the setting of the pericope. The discourses between Jesus of Nazareth and Jews take place in the context of the synagogue. This would have been highly improbable after the destruction of the Jerusalem Temple because there was greater caution in synagogues. The Twelfth

---

[30] Werner Georg Kümmel, *Introduction to the New Testament*, trans. Howard Clark Kee (Nashville: Abingdon Press, 1975), pp. 110-111.
[31] Theodore Stylianopoulos, *Justin Martyr and the Mosaic Law* (Missoula: Scholars Press, 1975).

Benediction of the Eighteen Benedictions which compels putting out of synagogue heretics, including Christians, clearly indicate an aggressive position of Jewish synagogues.[32] Given the destruction of the Jerusalem Temple, Jewish places of worship were cautious and would not have allowed an unknown person to read from the Bible and give a sermon. Although we are not sure when Eighteen Benedictions originated, it was most likely in place by the time shortly after the destruction of the Jerusalem Temple, if not earlier.[33] Given the unlikelihood for such a synagogue discourse, particularly of this kind after the destruction of the Jerusalem Temple, the whole framework of the Lukan pericope militates against post-70 AD provenance for this pericope.

Furthermore, I would argue that the original core of this Lukan pericope is dated before the death of Jesus of Nazareth in Jerusalem. If this pericope was composed right after the death of Jesus of Nazareth in Jerusalem but before the destruction of the Jerusalem Temple, then there would have been a greater anti-Jerusalem rhetoric or a greater anti-Jerusalem religious establishment hints. As it is, none of that exists. Rather, the conflict here resides with Galileans. Even the rejection of prophet idea (Luke 4:24) is referred to in the Galilean context, rather than the Jerusalem context.

I would state that the Lukan pericope is from the time of Jesus of Nazareth. There are several compelling reasons for this. First of all, this pericope satisfies the criterion of difference. Jesus of Nazareth represented in the Lukan pericope is vastly different from other religious leaders, including Galilean charismatics, who addressed Jews. They were more or less faithful to the core values of Judaism. One of the central core values in Judaism was the idea that Jews are a privileged people who are favored by God. As the Lukan pericope shows, Jesus of Nazareth differed from this position. The sermon found in Luke 4:24-27 shows that Jesus of Nazareth preached a sermon that illustrated that Elijah and Elisha, two great prophets of Israel, ministered to Gentiles and ignored the Jews. The implication of this sermon of Jesus of Nazareth is that Jews are not the favored people of God and God can prefer Gentitles. This idea would have been odious to a Jew living at the time of Jesus of Nazareth. This pericope satisfies the criterion of difference to illustrate that this pericope belongs to the Sitz im Leben of Jesus of Nazareth.

Furthermore, Luke 4:14-40 pericope satisfies the critierion of multiple attestation. This pericope is multiply attested in Mark 1:14-15 and Mark 6:1-6.[34]

---

[32] Filson, p. 303.

[33] Becker believes that the Eighteen Benedictions achieved their formal structure after 70 AD (p. 269).

[34] Kimball notes that Luke is using his unique L source and that explains why much of the Lukan material is not paralleled in Mark (p. 98). F. Bovon asserts that although Luke knew Mark 6:1-6, he used a different traditional source (in Q or S^{Lk}) where the Old Testament citation, its explanation, the sermon regarding Elijah and Elisha and the attack of the synagogue attendees of Jesus of Nazareth (Luke 4:29) had already been

Mark 1:14-15 corresponds to Luke 4:14-15. In both parts, Jesus of Nazareth is preaching in the Galilee area. Rest of the Lukan pericope corresponds to Mark 6:1-6. The framework of both pericopes are very similar. They both take place in a synagogue. In both pericopes, Jesus of Nazareth teaches in the synagogue. There is also commonality in the audience being impressed by teachings of Jesus of Nazareth. Furthermore, both pericopes show that Jesus of Nazareth is identified as a local person. And in both instances, Jesus of Nazareth expresses consternation that prophet is rejected in his hometown. Out of the two pericopes, the Markan one is shorter than the Lukan one.

There are some differences to be sure. The Markan pericope misses the detailed Bible-reading and the detailed sermon. Furthermore, the Markan version does not have the Jews of the synagogue organizing in mob violence to kill Jesus of Nazareth right after the sermon. It is not entirely impossible that both Mark and Luke share a common source but Mark chose to exclude some portions in lieu of his emphasis. Comparison between the Markan pericope and the Lukan pericope shows that Mark does have a different emphasis. In Markan pericope, what is stressed is Jesus of Nazareth's relationship to people. For instance, whereas the Lukan pericope only mentions a person asking a simple question: "Isn't this Joseph's son?" (Luke 4:22); the Markan pericope has a question that identifies Jesus of Nazareth more specifically: "Isn't this the carpenter? Isn't this Mary's son and the brother of James, Joseph, Judas and Simon? Aren't his sisters here with us?" (Mark 6:3). Markan concern for specificity in identification is also highlighted in another difference between the Lukan pericope and the Markan pericope. In the Lukan pericope, Jesus of Nazareth merely says: "No prophet is accepted in his hometown" (Luke 4:24). However, in the Markan pericope, Jesus of Nazareth says: "Only in his hometown, among his relatives and in his own house is a prophet without honor" (Mark 6:4). The difference between the Markan pericope and the Lukan pericope can be seen as one of emphasis. In other words, both of the pericopes relate to the same event, or story.

Besides satisfying the critera of difference and multiple attestation, the Lukan pericope satisfies the criterion of coherence, thereby pointing to the Sitz im Leben of Jesus of Nazareth himself. The periscope, particularly the sermon of Jesus of Nazareth, coheres with his teaching as found in the early Christian documents. For instance, Jesus of Nazareth opposes Jewish laws, such as Sabbath-keeping (Luke 6:1-11), which is essential within Judaism. There are other laws of Judaism that Jesus of Nazareth opposes, such as purity laws. Jesus of Nazareth teaches against normative practices in Judaism that were valued by

---

incorporated (F. Bovon, *Das Evangelium nach Lukas. 1. Teilband Lk 1,1 – 9,50* <Zürich-Neukirchen: Benziger, 1989>, pp. 207-208). Bovon argues that Luke 4:14-30 was one unit and represents the reality where "Lukas vewendet hier traditionelles Material" (*Das Evangelium nach Lukas*, p. 214).

Jews holding to the Jewish religion.[35] His antagonistic attitude towards core values such as these in Judaism is consistent with his stance against the core value of privileging Jews over Gentiles as exhibited in the Nazareth sermon in the Lukan pericope. Besides the coherence in a type of anti-Judaism teaching position of Jesus of Nazareth, Jesus of Nazareth's sermon in Luke 4 corresponds to his general ministry. Jesus of Nazareth ministered to Gentiles, such as the centurion (Luke 7:1-10). Furthermore, Jesus of Nazareth reached out to the outcasts of Jewish society, who were seen by religious Jews to be impure or somehow in violation of the Jewish law (Luke 5:12-17; 8:40-56). Historians of early Christianity often refer to this practice of Jesus of Nazareth as Open Table Fellowship.[36] It would certainly not be inaccurate to say that Open Table Fellowship was a central position of the Jesus movement, which put him in direct opposition to Judaism of his time. The sermon in Luke 4 certainly is harmonious with the principles of Open Table Fellowship that aggressively sought to include outcast of Judaism in the Jesus movement, such as the Samaritans, Gentiles, and the ritually impure.

In this light, it is clear to see that Jesus of Nazareth's sermon (Luke 4:24-27) was intentionally meant to offend the Jews. The two examples, of Elijah and Elisha, come from the book of Kings: 1 Kings 17:1-18:2 and 2 Kings 5:1-19. 1 Kings 17:1-18:2 relate to Luke 4:25-26, and 2 Kings 5:1-19 relate to Luke 4:27. First, we will examine 1 Kings 17:1-18:2, the Old Testament passage about Elijah[37] and the widow.[38] Jesus of Nazareth's sermon in the Lukan pericope presents the Old Testament account as if it was Elijah who saved the widow and it was intentional that Elijah go and save the Gentile widow and not any of the widows of Israel. The intentional pro-Gentile and anti-Israel texture is not found in the surface reading of the Old Testament account. When we look at 1 Kings 17:1-18:2, it seems like it was actually for Elijah's sake that he was sent to the widow. 1 Kings 17:7 states that brook had dried up because of no rain. This brook was the place that provided Elijah with water (1 Kings 17:6). Then, God gives Elijah direction so that he would not die: "Go at once to Zarephath of

---

[35] Enslin, pp. 117-118.

[36] Becker tries to emphasize the continuity of Open Table Fellowship by stating that it is like Isaiah 25:6 (p. 162). However, the biggest problem with this is that none of the Jewish sects of the time would have agreed that it represented continuity. They would have seen Jesus of Nazareth's practices as strange and a violation of the Law.

[37] Marsha C. White believes that "the historical Elijah was a legendary rain-inducer, similar to Honi the Circle-drawer..." (*The Elijah Legends and Jehu's Coup* <Atlanta: Scholars Press, 1997>, p. 32).

[38] Steven L. McKenzie argues that the Elijah and the widow story in 1 Kings 17 is derived from the story of Elisha found in 2 Kings 4 (*The Trouble with Kings: The Composition of the Book of Kings in the Deuteronomistic History* <Leiden: E. J. Brill, 1991>, p. 82).

Sidon and stay there. I have commanded a widow in that place to supply you with food" (1 Kings 17:9).

The narrative confirms the idea that the Old Testament account pictures Elijah as being rescued by the widow. Elijah goes to Zarephath as he was commanded by God, and when he is at the town gate area, he spots a widow gathering sticks. Assuming that she's the widow that God told him about, Elijah asks her to bring him water in a jar so that he may have something to drink (Luke 17:10). The fact that Elijah asks for water is significant because it highlights the fact that it was on account of the brook drying up that Elijah had to move. Furthermore, Elijah asking for water first is significant because God had told Elijah that He had commanded a widow to provide with him with food. But there is no mention of water. The fact that he asks for water first highlights the fact that because the brook dried up, it was the need for water that compelled the move and not the food. It can be inferred from the text that the ravens could have continued to provide Elijah with food as before (1 Kings 17:6).

But of course, Elijah asks for some food as well. But it is important to note that he does not ask for food before he asks for water. Furthermore, he does not ask for food as he is asking for water; that is, at the same time. The Old Testament account is clear in showing that the request for food followed the request for water. 1 Kings 17:11 states: "As she was going to get it [water], he called, 'And bring me, please, a piece of bread." The waw-consecutives (ותלך֯ס֯ויקרא) clearly show the sequential order of events. Furthermore, the use of ויקרא denotes calling out or shouting after the widow was on her way to get water.[39] The verse gives the impression that Elijah wanted the assurance that the widow would give him water before asking for food that she may have. Even the language, "please bring" or "please take" (לקחי־נא) is one of tender request. Qil (קיל) states: "ואין 'נא' אלא לשון בקשה"[40] The widow's reply is interesting. She denies that she has enough food for him. The widow says that she only has enough food for one meal for herself and her son.[41] After this meal, she and her son will die (1 Kings 17:12). The implication is that they will die of hunger because they will have eaten their last food. This reply causes the reader to question whether Elijah has the right widow.[42] It is more than possible that there

---

[39] Qil notes: "בהליכה לקחת את המים" (p. שנז), [1989, הוצאת מוסר הרב קוק, ירושלים: [מלכים א (יהודה קיל, ספר)

[40] קיל, מלכים ספר א, שנז p.

[41] John Gray emphasizes that the woman was poor and argues against Montgomery (p. 295) by stating that the upper chamber should be seen as a flimsy shelter not unlike those commonly seen on the flat roof tops of an Arab peasants' houses. It was meant to accommodate guests without infringing on family privacy and was necessary for Semitic convention of hospitality to avoid embarrassment (John Gray, *I & II Kings: A Commentary* <Philadelphia: The Westminster Press, 1963>, p. 341).

[42] Medieval Jewish commentator Rashi, commenting on 1 Kings 17:10, states that Elijah did not recognize the widow about whom God told him. Rashi refers to Genesis 24:15

were a number of widows in the place, and the narrative does not show Elijah questioning to see if the widow he was addressing was the right widow. This question is raised because 1 Kings 17:9 seems to indicate that God had already commanded a widow to give food to Elijah.

When the widow refuses to give Elijah food, he gives her the prophecy from God that she will not run out of flour or oil until the drought ends (1 Kings 17:14). The widow trusts Elijah and gives him bread. And the prophecy came true, so that Elijah, the widow, and her son ate food everyday (1 Kings 17:15). This account indicates that Elijah saved the widow in order to save himself. In fact, the Old Testament account seems to show that Elijah did not go to save the widow, but rather himself.[43] However, when she did not have enough food to save him, he prophesied for more food, so that he will have food to eat. Furthermore, it is important to note that Elijah needed the widow to prepare the bread from flour and oil. It is not certain if Elijah knew how to prepare food, himself. He could not have just eaten flour with oil. Elijah, indeed, needed the widow to prepare bread for him every day out of flour and oil. Because Elijah needed her, he prophesied the multiplication of flour and oil that also fed her and her son.

While the widow was important, her son was not as important. He was not needed to prepare Elijah food or provide Elijah with any needed services. The expandability of the son is highlighted in his sickness and death (1 Kings 17:17). Elijah could have left him dead. After all, by the widow's previous admission, they would have died of starvation anyway. It was because Elijah prophesied multiplication of flour and oil, that his life was prolonged. However, the widow ignores this fact and blames Elijah for the death. She cries out to Elijah: "What do you have against me, man of God? Did you come to remind me of my sin and kill my son?" (1 Kings 17:18). It was only because of her entreaty that Elijah prayed on the dead boy's behalf. The prayer of Elijah is important. Elijah prays to God: "O LORD my God, have you brought tragedy also upon this widow I am staying with, by causing her son to die?" (1 Kings 17:20). Elijah is bringing his case before God. He is complaining to God. Elijah is saying that he was shown kindness, hospitality, and support by the widow. He is saying to God that he is placed in a bind because the person who is supporting him has suffered a grave tragedy. Even in this prayer, we detect a selfish concern on the part of Elijah. He needed the woman to prepare bread for him. Now, she has

---

and points out that Elijah learned from the example of Eliezer, the servant of Abraham, in identifying the woman who gives the water as the woman referred to by God (*I Kings: A New Translation*, trans. Reuven Hochberg and A. J. Rosenberg <New York: The Judaica Press, Inc., 1984>, p. 179).

[43] B. J. Koet writes: "This was not meant as a rejection of Israel. On the contrary, it is a chance for the prophet to stay alive so that he can later restore the covenant between God and Israel (cf. 1 Kgs 18,31)" (*Five Studies on Interpretation of Scripture in Luke-Acs* <Leuven: Leuven University Press, 1989>, p. 46).

experienced tragedy and was nagging Elijah and making his life difficult. Elijah complains to God about the predicament he was in as the result of widow's son's death and the widow's sorrow. Elijah thus cries out to God: "O LORD my God, let this boy's life return to him!" (1 Kings 17:21). This prayer can be seen as a demand by God's prophet to God to improve his situation vis-à-vis the widow who was feeding him daily. There really is not a concern for the dead boy. This is clear when the dead boy is resurrected from the dead as the result of Elijah's prayer. Elijah was not excited in any way or showed any interest in the boy; he was insignificant to Elijah. What Elijah did was to bring the resurrected boy down to his mother (it is significant that the text uses the term "mother" (לאמו "to his mother") rather than "widow" (אשה אלמנה) or "woman" (אשה) in 1 Kings 17:23). And Elijah merely says to the widow in a matter-of-fact way: "Look, your son is alive!" (1 Kings 17:23). Basically, Elijah is saying that the widow's son was alive and that he did not want to hear her complaining any more.

All throughout the Old Testament account of Elijah and the Gentile widow, there is no real intentioned purpose of salvation for Gentiles or the Gentile widow.[44] He seems to stumble across this widow, whom he ended up giving a positive prophecy for in order that he might be fed and live. Elijah saves the life of the widow's boy not because he had any mission to Gentiles or wanted to resurrect his life. It was an act out of necessity since he was beholden to the generosity of the widow and needed her to continue feeding him. Elijah was merely trying to make his own life better by ending the nagging. The picture that Jesus of Nazareth gives in the Lukan pericope is quite different. The sermon basically states that Elijah purposely avoided Israelite widows and went to a Gentile widow to save her. The implication is, of course, that God favored Gentiles over Jews. Those in the synagogue who were acquainted with the story certainly would have been offended by the spin that Jesus of Nazareth was putting on the Old Testament account. What would have been worse in the minds of the Jewish[45] listeners was that the spin was aggressively anti-Jewish and pro-Gentile.

---

[44] In fact, James A. Montgomery points out that Elijah was in Zarephath to be out of the reach of King Ahab, to whom he had uttered the prophecy of the famine in 1 Kings 17:1 (*A Critical and Exegetical Commentary on the Book of Kings* <Edinburgh: T. & T. Clark, 1951>, p. 294). In other words, Elijah was there for his own protection.

[45] James Richard Linville notes: "The uncertainties surrounding the rise of the set of cultural signifiers which are now regarded as 'Judaism,' and the dangers of anachronistic judgments on what constituted a normative, or collective 'Judaism' in the Persian period makes the simple substitution of 'Judaean' with 'Jew' extremely difficult at best" (*Israel in the Book of Kings: The Past as a Project of Social Identity* <Sheffield: Sheffield Academic Press, 1998>, p. 26).

Similar trend seems to be operating with Jesus of Nazareth's interpretation of 2 Kings 5:1-19, the story of Elisha and Naaman[46] who has leprosy. The Old Testament account is not explicitly pro-Gentile. We find Naaman, a commander in the army of the king of Aram, with leprosy (2 Kings 5:1). His wife has an Israelite slave[47] who tells her that a prophet in her country could cure Naaman of his leprosy (2 Kings 5:2-3). Naaman goes with the blessing of the king of Aram, armed with his letter[48] and much wealth as reward (2 Kings 5:5). When Naaman reaches Israel and gives the letter from king of Aram, the king of Israel tears his clothes because he thinks that the king of Aram is trying to start a war with Israel[49] by using Naaman as an excuse (2 Kings 5:7). Elisha hears about the torn robes of the king of Israel and sends him a message: "Why have you torn your robes? Have the man come to me and he will know that there is a prophet in Israel" (2 Kings 5:8). From the Old Testament narrative, we can deduce two reasons why Elisha sends for Naaman. First of all, it is clearly stated in the text that Elisha wants to show off that there is a prophet in Israel; namely, himself. Second of all, Elisha is dismayed that the king of Israel has torn his clothes and is moping around scared of what he perceived as the imminent invasion of king of Aram because of Naaman. Elisha does not seem particularly interested in healing Naaman. And there certainly is not an emphasis that Elisha wanted to heal a Gentile rather than Jews.

Elisha's nonchalant attitude toward Naaman is further emphsized in the encounter between Elisha and Naaman. In fact, there really is not an encounter because when Naaman reaches Elisha, Elisha does not go out to meet him. Rather, Elisha sends his servant with instructions. As if this were not insult enough, the instruction directs Naaman to wash himself seven times in the

---

[46] Montgomery states that Naaman's name was "good Syrian" and that it is multiply attested in that it appears in Ugaritic tablets (p. 373). Qil (קיל) notes that the name and its derivative forms are found in Israel as well (p. תקג [1989, הוצאת מוסר הרב קוק :ירושלים] ב (יהודה קיל, ספר מלכים)

[47] The Israelite slave girl is called נערה קטנה in Hebrew. Medieval Jewish commentator Radak explains that according to *peshat*, the girl was at the beginning of *naaruth*, which lasts six months from the age of 12 (*II Kings: A New English Translation*, trans. A. J. Rosenberg <New York: The Judaica Press, Inc., 1980>, p. 271).

[48] Montgomery notes that letters requesting international (medical) courtesy was not uncommon in the ancient world and gives the example of a long letter by Hattushil, king of Hittites, to Kadashmanturgu, king of Babylon (ca. 1275 BC) about the whereabouts of a Babylonian physician sent to the Hittite court (p. 374). Also, Gray states that in the Amarna tablets, Tušratta of Mitanni writes a letter to Amenhotep III stating that he has sent the statue of Astarte of Nineveh with healing powers to the Pharaoh as it has been done in previous generations (p. 453).

[49] Gray notes that the time was one in which there was uneasy peace between Aram with its capital in Damascus and Israel (p. 453). Rick Dale Moore writes: "Aram is obviously in a position of military superiority" (*God Saves: Lessons from the Elisha Stories* <Sheffield: Sheffield Academic Press, 1990>, p. 72).

Jordan and then his leprosy will be healed. Naaman felt the insult and exclaims: "I thought that he would surely come out to me and stand and call on the name of the LORD his God, wave his hand over the spot and cure me of my leprosy. Are not Abana and Pharpar, the rivers of Damascus, better than any of the waters of Israel? Couldn't I wash in them and be cleansed?" (2 Kings 5:11-12). In his anger, Naaman walked off. Elisha and his servants do not try to stop Naaman from going away not healed. Elisha and his servants do not seem too concerned about Naaman being healed. It was Naaman's servants who persuade Naaman to take the dips in the Jordan River (2 Kings 5:13) The result of the dips was that Naaman was healed of leprosy (2 Kings 5:14).

Naaman goes back to Elisha and declares that God of Israel is the only God and that he would worship no other (2 Kings 5:15). Then, Naaman tries to persuade Elisha to take the gifts that he brought, but Elisha wants none of it (2 Kings 5:16). This part of the story illustrates a few important points. First of all, the fact that Naaman accepts the God of Israel as his God show the triumph of God of Israel over God of Aram. Rick Dale Moore writes: "A theological victory has been won. Naaman has come under the authority of Yahweh. Thus the submission of Naaman is complete. Israel has prevailed on all levels: personal, national, and theological."[50] In fact, Naaman even apologizes in advance if he is compelled to bow down to his country's deity as the result of the king of Aram leaning on his arm (2 Kings 5:18). This is revelling in the victory of God of Israel over God of Aram. This victory represents on a certain level, victory of Israel over Aram. Thus, in stark contrast to king of Israel in distress at impending war with king of Aram, Elisha stands regal like a king to whom Naaman, king of Aram's right hand man pays homage. Elisha of the Old Testament narrative is the hero of the story. The important point, of course, is that Elisha has won a point for the Israelites. Elisha was not there to heal a Gentile, but he was there to save Israel's honor, take away the disgrace of the king of Israel, and show God of Israel to be supreme.

The sermon of Jesus of Nazareth certainly gives an opposite rendering than the surface reading of the Old Testament narrative on which the sermon is based. Jesus of Nazareth preaches as if God intended to save the Gentile and ignore the Israelites. Charles A. Kimball writes: "These Elijah/Elisha allusions also foreshadow both the Jews' continued rejection of Jesus and the church's ministry in Acts (i.e., the Gentile mission), thus the programmatic nature of the narrative. Therefore, they not only picture Jesus' ministry as antitypical to these experiences of Elijah and Elisha but also give a justification from the OT for the Gentile mission."[51] In fact, Jesus of Nazareth flatly states: "And there were

---

[50] Moore, p. 80.
[51] Kimball, p. 115. Alfred Plummer writes: "They see the point of His illustrations; He has been comparing them to those Jews who were judged less worthy of Divine benefits than the heathen" (*A Critical and Exegetical Commentary on the Gospel according to S. Luke* [Edinburgh: T. & T. Clark, 1922], pp. 128-129).

many in Israel with leprosy in the time of Elisha the prophet, yet not one of them was cleansed – only Naaman the Syrian" (Luke 4:27). The Old Testament narrative did not mention that there were a lot of Israelites with leprosy. It could just as well been, but the important point is that the Old Testament narrative does not mention that. Further significant is that the Old Testament account does not mention that not one Israelite was healed of leprosy. In fact, certain part of the Old Testament narrative seems to gravitate against this. In 2 Kings 5:3, the Israelite slave tells the wife of Naaman: "If only my master could see the prophet who is in Samaria! He would cure him of his leprosy." How did this Israelite woman know that Elisha could heal those with leprosy? There is high probability that he had healed some Israelites with leprosy, so that she knew that he is able to do this. If this is correct, then, the Old Testament passage would seem to stand against Jesus of Nazareth's sermon which is very anti-Jewish.

How can we explain the extreme anti-Jewish position found in the Nazareth sermon of Jesus of Nazareth? I would argue that it is because Jesus of Nazareth wanted to set his movement apart from Judaism from the very beginning. In a sense, therefore, there was a self-awareness of distinction and opposition from the earliest Sitz im Leben of the Jesus movement.

Bibliography

Bachmann, Michael. *Jerusalem und der Tempel: Die geographisch-theologischen Elemente in der lukanischen Sicht des jüdischen Kultzentrums*. Stuttgart: Verlag W. Kohlhammer, 1980.

Becker, Jürgen. *Jesus of Nazareth*. Translated by James E. Crouch. New York: Walter de Gruyter, 1998.

Bornkamm, Günther. *Jesus of Nazareth*. Translated by Irene and Fraser McLuskey with James M. Robinson. New York: Harper & Brothers Publishers, 1960.

Bovon, François. *Luke the Theologian: Thirty-three Years of Research (1950-1983)*. Translated by Ken McKinney. Allison Park: Pickwick Publications, 1978.

Bovon, François. *Das Evangelium nach Lukas. 1. Teilband Lk 1,1 – 9,50*. Zürich-Neukirchen: Benziger, 1989.

Bruce, F. F. *New Testament History*. Garden City: Doubleday & Company, Inc., 1971.

Burchard, Christophe. "Jesus of Nazareth." *Christian Beginnings: Word and Community from Jesus to Post-Apostolic Times*. Edited by Jürgen Becker. Translated by Annemarie S. Kidder and Reinhard Krauss. Louisville: Westminster/John Knox Press, 1993. Pages 15-72.

Conzelmann, Hans. *The Theology of St. Luke*. Translated by Geoffrey Buswell. Philadelphia: Fortress Press, 1982.

Crossan, John Dominic. *The Historical Jesus: The Life of a Mediterranean Jewish Peasant*. San Francisco: HarperSanFrancisco, 1991.

Dunn, James D. G. *A New Perspective on Jesus: What the Quest for the Historical Jesus Missed*. Grand Rapids: Baker Academic, 2005.

Ehrman, Bart D. *Jesus: Apocalyptic Prophet of the New Millennium*. New York: Oxford University Press, 1999.

Enslin, Morton Scott. *The Prophet from Nazareth*. New York: McGraw-Hill Book Company, Inc., 1961.

Filson, Floyd V. *A New Testament History: The Story of the Emerging Church*. Philadelphia: The Westminister Press, 1964.

Flusser, David. *Jesus*. Translated by Ronald Walls. New York: Herder and Herder, 1969.

Gowler, David B. *Host, Guest, Enemy, and Friend: Portrait of the Pharisees in Luke and Acts*. New York: Peter Lang, 1991.

Grant, Michael. *Jesus: An Historian's Review of the Gospels*. New York: Charles Scribner's Sons, 1977.

Gray, John. *I & II Kings: A Commentary*. Philadelphia: The Westminster Press, 1963.

Gutherie, Donald. *A Shorter Life of Christ*. Grand Rapids: Zondervan Publishing House, 1970.

Holtz, Traugott. *Untersuchungen über die alttestamentlichen Zitate bei Lukas*. Berlin: Akademie Verlag, 1968.

Jeremias, Joachim. *Die Sprache des Lukasevangeliums: Redaktion und Tradition im Nicht-Markusstoff des dritten Evangeliums*. Gottingen: Vandenhoeck & Ruprecht, 1980.

Kimball, Charles A. *Jesus' Exposition of the Old Testament in Luke's Gospel*. Sheffield: Sheffield Academic Press, 1994.

Kingsbury, Jack Dean. *Conflict in Luke: Jesus, Authorities, Disciples*. Minneapolis: Fortress Press, 1991.

Koet, B. J. *Five Studies on Interpretation of Scripture in Luke-Acts*. Leuven: Leuven University Press, 1989.

Kümmel, Werner Georg. *Introduction to the New Testament*. Translated by Howard Clark Kee. Nashville: Abingdon Press, 1975.

Linville, James Richard. *Israel in the Book of Kings: The Past as a Project of Social Identity*. Sheffield: Sheffield Academic Press, 1998.

Lohse, Eduard. *The New Testament Environment*. Translated by John E. Steely. Nashville: Abingdon, 1976.

Malherbe, Abraham J. *Social Aspects of Early Christianity*. Baton Rouge: Louisiana State University Press, 1977.

Marshall, I. Howard. *Luke: Historian and Theologian*. Sydney: The Paternoster Press, 1970.

McKenzie, Steven L. *The Trouble with Kings: The Composition of the Book of Kings in the Deuteronomistic History*. Leiden: E. J. Brill, 1991.

Meeks, Wayne A. *The First Urban Christians: The Social World of the Apostle Paul*. New Haven: Yale University Press, 1983.

Montgomery, James A. *A Critical and Exegetical Commentary on the Books of Kings.* Edinburgh: T. & T. Clark, 1951.

Moore, Rick Dale. *God Saves: Lessons from the Elisha Stories.* Sheffield: Sheffield Academic Press, 1990.

Neirynck, F. (Editor). *L'Évangile de Luc.* Leuven: Leuven University Press, 1989.

Plummer, Alfred. *A Critical and Exegetical Commentary on the Gospel according to S. Luke.* Edinburgh: T. & T. Clark, 1922.

Ravens, David. *Luke and the Restoration of Israel.* Sheffield: Sheffield Academic Press, 1995.

Schweitzer, Albert. *The Quest for the Historical Jesus: A Critical Study of Its Progess from Reimarus to Wrede.* Translated by W. Montgomery. New York: MacMillan Publishing Co., Inc., 1968.

Shaw, George. *The Conflict of Jesus.* Boston: Richard G. Badger, 1916.

Snowden, James H. *Jesus as Judged by His Enemies: A Study of the Criticisms and Attacks Made on Jesus by His Enemies.* New York: The Abingdon Press, 1922.

Stylianopoulos, Theodore G. *Justin Martyr and the Mosaic Law.* Missoula: Scholars Press, 1975

Theissen, Gerd. *Social Reality and the Early Christians: Theology, Ethics, and the World of the New Testament.* Translated by Margaret Kohl. Minneapolis: Fortress Press, 1992.

Theissen, Gerd. *The Shadow of the Galilean: The Quest of the Historical Jesus in Narrative Form.* Translated by John Bowden. London: SCM Press, Ltd, 1987.

Tiede, David L. *Prophecy and History in Luke-Acts.* Philadelphia: Fortress Press, 1980.

White, Marsha C. *The Elijah Legends and Jehu's Coup.* Atlanta: Scholars Press, 1997.

-----, *I Kings: A New English Translation.* Translated by Reuven Hochberg and A. J. Rosenberg. New York: The Judaica Press, Inc., 1984.

-----, *II Kings: A New English Translation.* Translated by A. J. Rosenberg. New York: The Judaica Press, Inc., 1980.

יהודה קיל. ספר מלכים א. ירושלים: הוצאת מוסר הרב קוק, 1989.

יהודה קיל. ספר מלכים ב. ירושלים: הוצאת מוסר הרב קוק, 1989.

"The Psalms of Solomon as a Pro-Zadokite Document: A Content-Thematic Examination of Chapter 17"

The Psalms of Solomon[1] is a quintessential Late Second Temple Period document that represents the views of practically all Jews of the Late Second Temple Period, who called themselves Jews.[2] However, it is important to recognize the distinctively pro-Zadokite nature of the Psalms of Solomon. The psalm that best exhibits this is chapter 17. Psalms of Solomon 17 reads like pro-Zadokite propaganda. The pro-Zadokite propaganda is achieved by the poet's[3] amalgamating several genre categories; namely, history, apology, and the apocalyptic.

The historic portion is found primarily in the first part of Psalms of Solomon 17. Most prominently, the historical portion is visible in Psalms of Solomon 17:5-22. It is no surprise that the historical portion clearly exhibits a pro-Zadokite bias. How is this evident? The historical portion starts with King David, who is attributed with the line of monarchy that instituted Zadokites[4] as

---

[1] For a good examination of various extant manuscripts, see Robert R. Hann, *The Manuscript History of the Psalms of Solomon* (Chico: Scholars Press, 1982).

[2] See my monograph, *The Jerusalem Tradition in the Late Second Temple Period: Diachronic and Synchronic Developments Surrounding Psalms of Solomon 11* (Lanham: University Press of America, 2007).

[3] Kim, Heerak Christian, *Hebrew, Jewish, and Early Christian Studies: Academic Essays* (Cheltenham: The Hermit Kingdom Press, 2005), p. 2.

[4] Sigmund Mowinckel writes: "There are even signs that point to a connexion between the new priestly family to whom David entrusted the Yahweh cult in the Temple–the Zadokites–and the ancient dynasty of priest kings in Jerusalem" (Sigmund Mowinckel, *The Psalms in Israel's Worship*, tr. James L. Crenshaw <Grand Rapids: William B. Eerdmans Publishing Company, 2004>, p. 36).

the high priests of the Jerusalem Temple. Privileging of the Davidic line[5] was synonymous with privileging of the Zadokite priesthood. Since it was the line of David that built the First Jerusalem Temple and instituted the Zadokite line as the legitimate high priestly line, it was only natural to see pro-David ideology as coupled with pro-Zadokite ideology. In a sense, emphasizing the kingship of David and his line was a way to emphasize the legitimacy of Zadokite priesthood. They can be seen as the flip-side of the same coin. A person who would acknowledge and emphasize the kingship of David's line would naturally emphasize the value of Zadokite high priests. Thus, it is no surprise that the poet-composer of the Psalms of Solomon, who was a Zadokite priest himself, would privilege the Davidic royal line and emphasize that. In fact, in the mini-history of Israel in Psalms of Solomon 17, the poet-composer starts with King David and not with any other significant figure in the history of Israel, such as Abraham and Adam. This must be seen as strategic on the part of the composer of the Psalms of Solomon.

Indeed, the historical portion of Psalms of Solomon 17, found in verses 5 to 22, starts with King David. Psalms of Solomon 17:5 proclaims: "Thou, O LORD, didst choose David to be king over Israel, and didst swear unto him touching his seed for ever, that his kingdom should not fail before thee."[6] The poet-composer of the Psalms of Solomon is emphatic in divine sanction of David's royal line. It was God who chose David king over Israel. Not only did God choose David as king, it was God who swore to make his descendants kings, forever. The fact that the poet-composer stresses the oath-making aspect of God is significant. In a sense, God covenanted with King David to make his descendants king, forever. Not only did God promise to uphold the royal line of David and his descendants, He promised to protect the kingdom of David. The poet-composer of the Psalms of Solomon is not ambiguous at all about the legitimacy of the Davidic royal line.[7]

Of course, given that this is a Late Second Temple Period document, it would not be hard to anticipate the question of the readers for whom this document was composed. Why was it that there was no longer the Davidic royal line on the throne of Israel? Could it be possible that the Davidic line was not the legitimate royal line for Israel? Anticipating such questions from his readers, the poet-composer of the Psalms of Solomon exonerates the royal line of David from blame. Psalms of Solomon 17:6 argues: "But when we sinned,

---

[5] Marinus de Jonge writes: "The 17th and 18the Psalm [of Solomon] base their hope on the house of David from which an ideal, God-pleasing king would be born" (Marinus de Jonge, "The Future in the Psalms of Solomon" in *Jewish Eschatology, Early Christian Christology and the Testament of the Twelve Patriarch* <Leiden: E. J. Brill, 1991, pp. 3-27>, pp. 5-6).

[6] See in the Old Testament: 2 Samuel 7; Psalm 89:4-5.

[7] Cf. John J. Collins, *Apocalypticism in the Dead Sea Scrolls* (London: Routledge, 1997), p. 79.

sinners rose up against us; they fell upon us and thrust us out: even they, to whom thou madest no promise, took away our place with violence." It is clear who is blamed, here. The people[8] are being blamed for what happened to the Davidic line and to Israel. It was not the fault of King David, King Saul, or any of the members of the royal line of David that the complete destruction of Israel and the ensuing Exile happened. The fault is blamed on the people. In the process, the royal line of David is completely cleared of any blame. This is different from the emphasis found in the Old Testament. The Old Testament, while putting blame on people of Israel, does not exonerate the royal line of David. In fact, the Old Testament blames the royal Davidic line. For instance, King Solomon had many foreign wives. False religions entered through his foreign wives. In fact, it was the royal line of David that encouraged idolatry and false religion. It was the active encouragement of the descendants of David who ruled in the thrones of Israel and Judah who intentionally went away from God and proper worship of God. This is the blame of the Old Testament. But the composer of the Psalms of Solomon, being a Zadokite[9] and wanting to encourage pro-Zadokite support, intentionally veers away from any mire of accusation that David and his line would fall into. It was the people and not David's descendants who caused God's judgement on Israel. It is clear why the composer of the Psalms of Solomon does this. The poet-composer of the Psalms

---

[8] George W. E. Nickelsburg argues that Psalms of Solomon 17:6-8 is blaming the Hasmoneans directly for usurping the throne (George W. E. Nickelsburg, *Jewish Literature between the Bible and the Mishnah: A Historical and Literary Introduction* <Philadelphia: Fortress Press, 1981>, p. 207).

[9] I am somewhat original in arguing for the Zadokite nature of the author. However, scholars have argued that the author was reformist in nature and opposed the Temple leadership. For instance, Herbert E. Ryle and Montague R. James argued that the author was a Pharisee who was concerned with religious renewal (Herbert E. Ryle and Montague R. James, *Psalms of the Pharisees Commonly Called the Psalms of Solomon* <Eugene: Wipf & Stock Publishers, 2006>). However, their identification of the author as Pharisees is problematic because the Pharisees were not interested in propping up priestly power along with the Jerusalem Temple. In fact, they were largely in conflict with priestly groups, such as the Sadducees. Kenneth Atkinson takes a more generalist approach. He simply emphasizes that the author belonged to a reformist group of Jews, rather than that he was specifically Pharisaic. Atkinson writes: "The sinners constitute the most clearly discernible group within PsSol 17, for they stood in marked contrast to the psalmist's community. The author most frequently denounced this party under the rubrics of sinners (PsSol 17.5, 23, 25, 36), "they" (PsSol 17.6), "them" (PsSol 17.7, 8, 12, 15, 19), and "their" (PsSol 17.9, 24). These transgressors were clearly Jewish because the psalmist also called them the children of the contract (PsSol 17.15)" (Kenneth Atkinson, *An Intertextual Study of the Psalms of Solomon: Pseudepigrapha* <Lewiston: The Edwin Mellen Press, 2000>, pp. 334-335). I would argue that the group of reform minded Jews were reformist Zadokites who wanted proper cultic worship at the Jerusalem Temple. The author belonged to this group by lineage and also actively identified with them through his writing.

of Solomon knew that he needed to defend the royal line of David since it was this royal line who gave legitimacy to the Zadokite priestly line. To attack it would be counterproductive to pro-Zadokite propaganda, to defend it would be constructive to the goals of bringing the Zadokites back to the Jerusalem Temple as its religious leaders.

Psalms of Solomon 17:6 continues and describes that it was because "we sinned" (and not King David and his royal line), that sinners rose up against the Jews. By sinners, the poet-composer of Psalms of Solomon 17 refers to the Babylonians[10] who decimated Jerusalem's population, destroyed the Jerusalem Temple, and dismantled the nation. Psalms of Solomon 17:6 is clear in showing that this is referring to the Babylonian destruction because it refers to the Exile.[11] These so-called sinners came in and kicked the Jewish remnant out of Jerusalem. This point is reiterated within Psalms of Solomon 17:6. These people took away the place of the Jews with violence. The poet-composer of the Psalms of Solomon is emphatic in reminding his readers that those who took Jerusalem away from the Jews were not people of promise. The Babylonians were not a people to whom God had made any explicit promise. But it was these Babylonians with whom the LORD did not communicate that destroyed Jerusalem and exiled the Jews.

Psalms of Solomon 17:7 continues to remind the Jewish readers of the fact that the people who destroyed Jerusalem were not God's people in any way. Not only were these people not explicitly given any promise by God, they did not honor God in any way. Psalms of Solomon 17:7 states this explicitly. The people who destroyed Jerusalem were people who chose a kingdom that suited them and pleased them. They were not interested in having a kingdom that honored God. Of course, the contrast here is between the Davidic Kingdom which honored God and the unbelieving kingdom of the Babylonians which had no respect for God. It was this unbelieving nation, however, that destroyed Jerusalem. Verse 8 specifically mentions that the unbelieving kingdom destroyed King David's kingdom. Psalms of Solomon 17:8 states that the

---

[10] Atlhough Herbert E. Ryle and Montague R. James argue that "sinners" are Jews rather than Gentiles (pp. 129-130), they contradict themselves in that "sinner" in Psalms of Solomon 2:1 refers to a Gentile, namely Pompey (p. 6). The fact is that the poet-composer uses "sinners" for both Jews and Gentiles. This is consistent with Jewish eschatological language in the Late Second Temple Period. Marinus de Jonge writes: "The sinners are, in the first place, non-Jews who do not observe God's commandments, but who are used as instruments of God for the punishment of his people (Pss 2, 8, 17). But sinners are also found in Israel and their transgressions are the reason for God's intervention" (Marinus de Jonge, "The Psalms of Solomon" in *Outside the Old Testament*, ed. Marinus de Jonge <Cambridge: Cambridge University Press, 1985, pp. 159-177>, p. 160).

[11] It is important to remember the pervasiveness of the Babylonian Exile in the consciousness of the Exilic and Post-Exilic Jewish communities.

unbelieving nation destroyed the throne of David with shouts of triumph. When we read further in this verse, we see why the poet-composer mentioned the name of King David; it was in order to show that God still favored David.

Even though the kingdom of David and his descendants were destroyed by the unbelieving kingdom, God did not abandon David's line. Psalms of Solomon 17:8 describes God's judgement on the kingdom that destroyed the throne of David. God destroyed that kingdom and removed their royal line. Of course, the reference is to the overthrow of the Babylonian Empire by the Persian Empire. It is important to note here that the poet-composer of the Psalms of Solomon specifically indicates that God's overthrow of the Babylonian kingdom was because it destroyed the throne of David. For the poet, that was the gravest and most egregious sin committed by the Babylonians. The point is that the annihilation of the Jews, decimation of Jerusalem, and destruction of the nation was not as important as the ending of the throne of David; this is the poet's particular emphasis.

Given that the poet was a Zadokite priest engaging in pro-Zadokite propaganda, it is not surprising that he chooses this particular line of exposition. He was interested in proving that King David's line was the line chosen by God and documenting how God punished those who opposed that line. This was the case for the Babylonians who came in and destroyed the throne of David. It may be because of Israel's sins that Babylonians came in and destroyed Jerusalem, but it did not excuse the fact that they destroyed the line of David, chosen by God. It was their harming of the royal line of David that brought God's condemnation and judgment down on them. It was because of this transgression that God removed their royal line from the face of the earth.

Psalms of Solomon 17:9 describes that the one who brought down the royal line of the Babylonians was someone who was not Jewish. This is consistent with history and the collective memory of the Jews who read the Psalms of Solomon during the poet-composer's day. The Babylonian Empire was destroyed by the Persian Empire, which the Jews obviously considered foreign to their race in the Late Second Temple Period. But it was God who raised up a Gentile to destroy the Babylonian Empire. The implication, of course, is that just as God raised up a Gentile to destroy the Jews for their transgression against God, God raised up another Gentile to destroy those Gentiles who destroyed the kingdom of David. In a way, therefore, the poet-composer establishes the pattern of God's judgement in these few verses. God can and does raise up people with whom He does not communicate or offer any promises to accomplish His acts of judgment. This can be seen as a veiled threat by the poet-composer.

The poet-composer is warning the Jews of his day, particularly Jews in power that God can raise up any heathen nation to destroy the chosen nation and the chosen people because this is how God operates. God may destroy the nation that destroys them afterwards, but even in this case He may raise up another, different group of Gentiles to do so. In a sense, Jews are not needed for God's judgment even against the Gentiles who harm them. This veiled threat should be seen as a slight to the Hasmoneans. The Hasmoneans prided themselves in driving out the Syrians who defiled the Jerusalem Temple. In a sense, they derived their legitimacy from their triumph and military victory. The poet-composer is essentially saying that they have no reason to exult since God can even raise up Gentiles to accomplish His judgment. In fact, the Hasomeans should be careful since they have driven out the legitimate priests, the Zadokites from the Land. The Zadokites were the legitimate high priests of the Jerusalem Temple whom the throne of David and his seed chose. Bilzah Nitzan describes the gravity of the situation by identifying two crises in the Late Second Temple Period: "The first occurred when the priestly management of the Second Temple period inclined towards Hellenistic customs. The second crisis followed when the Zadokite priesthood was deprived of control of the Temple ritual by the Hasmonean priesthood."[12] Driving out the Zadokites was like destroying the throne of David. For this, the Hasmoneans will be judged. The explicitly pro-Davidic discourse in Psalms of Solomon 17:8 is meant to be anti-Hasmonean and pro-Zadokite. It was a part of the pro-Zadokite propaganda of the poet-composer of the Psalms of Solomon.

Psalms of Solomon 17:10-12 should be seen as an apologetic piece interwoven into the historical account. In these verses, the poet-composer of the Psalms of Solomon lays down a generic rule regarding how God operates in the world. God judges the evil-doers and blesses those who submit to Him.[13] God is righteous whatever happens. When people suffer and die, they experienced adversity because they had done something wrong. When people are saved, they are saved because of their faithfulness to God. Psalms of Solomon 17:10 emphasizes that God judges people according to their sins. In the context of the historical account, this can be seen as applicable both to the Jews who sinned and, therefore, brought upon themselves the judgement of God in the form of a successful Babylonian invasion and the ensuing destruction of Babylonians by the Persian Empire because the Babylonians destroyed the Davidic royal throne, which God had chosen. God punishes each people according to their sins against God. In the outlining of the general principle and apology for God in the destructions, the poet-composer, in essence, threatens the Hasmoneans with

---

[12] Bilhah Nitzan, "The Concept of the Covenant in Qumran Literature" in *Historical Perspectives: From Hasmoneans to Bar Kokhba in Light of the Dead Sea Scrolls: Proceedings of the Fourth International Symposium of the Orion Center for the Study of the Dead Sea Scrolls and Associated Literature, 27-31 January, 1999*, ed. David Goodblatt, Avital Pinnick, and Daniel R. Schwartz (Leiden: Brill, 2001, pp. 85-104), pp. 94-95.

[13] Joachim Schüpphaus, *Die Psalmen Salomos: Ein Jerusalemer Theologie und Frömmigkeit in der Mitte des vorchristlichen Jahrhunderts* (Leiden: E. J. Brill, 1977), pp. 83-84.

God's judgement for having driven out the priestly line appointed by the seed of David to be high priests of the Jerusalem Temple.

In a like manner, Psalms of Solomon 17:11 describes how and why God shows compassion on people. God blesses people because of what they do. God blesses people for their faithfulness to Him. This is a general principle that the poet-composer is laying down with the strategic purpose of propangandizing for the Zadokites. First of all, this is a form of proclamation that God will look after the Zadokites. The readers of the Psalms of Solomon were keenly aware that the Zadokites were displaced from the Jerusalem Temple. They assumed that that was their end. But the poet-composer of the Psalms of Solomon indicates that God will diligently seek them out and protect their seed as He has those who were doing good works for God. This can be seen as an apology for the Zadokites who had run off into the Dead Sea area and founded a rigid law-observant community in Qumran. Some Zadokites priests with their core group of followers went off into Qumran to await the judgement of God on the Hasmoneans. When God punishes them, the Zadokites from Qumran would return to Jerusalem and purify the Jerusalem Temple cult.[14] The poet-composer of the Psalms of Solomon, as a Zadokite himself, sides with the community at Qumran and their vision. However, it was not only the Zadokites in Qumran that the poet-composer of the Psalms of Solomon was defending; he also supported the Zadokites in Leontopolis, Egypt. He knew that they were in exile, not dissimilar to the Jews who went into exile in Babylon. Their exile was meant to be temporary and the poet-composer was hopeful that they would return soon and occupy their legitimate place in the Jerusalem Temple as the legitimate high priests and their attendants.

The three-verse apology for God and for the Zadokites concludes with the assurance that God is faithful in His judgement which extends to the whole earth (Psalms of Solomon 17:12). In a sense, this verse is meant as a promise to the Zadokites of their vengeance-is-mine-saith-the-LORD justice and their eventual restoration. This certainly was a coded way to encourage the Zadokites in exile – both in Qumran and in Leontopolis. Furthermore, this was meant as a veiled threat to the Hasomeans for having exiled the Zadokites, in effect.

Following the short apologetic excursus of Psalms of Solomon 17:10-12, the poet-composer of the Psalms of Solomon continues with his historical account. The coherent historical piece can be seen in Psalms of Solomon 17:13-22. However, this historical piece is not a continuation of the historical account which the poet-composer left off in Psalms of Solomon 17:9; rather, it is a reiteration of it in a sense. Psalms of Solomon 17:13-22, in fact, focuses on the divine punishment of Jerusalem in its destruction and the Exile. In this regard, it

---

[14] Hyuk Seung Kwon, *The Zion Tradition and the Kingdom of God: A Study on the Zion Traditions as Relevant to the Understanding of the Concept of the Kingdom of God in the New Testament* (Ph.D. thesis, Hebrew University of Jerusalem, 1998), pp. 172-173.

can be seen as an elaboration of the concept of the divine judgement of God. This seems logical given that Psalm of Solomon 17:10-12 was an excursus on the righteousness of God in punishing those who oppose Him and blessing those who support Him.[15]

Psalms of Solomon 17:13-22 is quite detailed in describing the divine judgement of Israel. Verse 13 describes the destruction as annihilation; it states: "The tempest hath laid waste our land that none should inhabit it." This is describing a military annihilation. In this destruction, young and old and their children are killed. In essence, the poet-composer recounts how the Babylonian army annihilated infants up to disabled elderly in their invasion and destruction of Jerusalem. There was a slaughter of the people in Jerusalem that resembled a thorough annihilation. Psalms of Solomon 17:14 shows that despite the massacre, there was a remnant left and this remnant was exiled to a far away land.[16] The poet-composer indicates that those exiled were political leaders. He states in verse 14: "And the princes of the land he turned into derision, and spared them not."

Psalms of Solomon 17:15 describes the ruler who was used by God as His instrument of judgment. The poet-composer is clear in stating that the chosen destroyer was an unbeliever. This unbelieving foreigner was the one who did much harm in Israel. Of course, he is describing King Nebuchadnezzar. The fact of his unbelieving status is specifically described in verse 15: "His heart was alien from our God." This is a very important point since there may be some Jews who believed that God chose King Nebuchadnezzar to destroy Jerusalem and Israel because somehow he was secretly a worshipper of God. Some may have supposed that God appointed him to destroy Jerusalem and annihilate the people because he was worthy of the role of being the executor of divine justice against the Jews and Israel. The poet-composer of the Psalms of Solomon is emphatic in denying any possibility of this; he describes the destroyer of Jerusalem and its temple and annihilator of Jews as completely an unbeliever. In a sense, the poet-composer upholds the Old Testament teaching about the

---

[15] "Briefly, because of a conviction that unquestioning compliance with God's commandments is the essence of religion, but also because of an expectation of divine reward or retribution. The prophetic idea of the Covenant concluded by God with his people was understood to mean that the people were to observe the Torah strictly and conscientiously, and God in return would pay the promised recompense, both to the nation and the individual Jew, for their good deeds and offenses" (Emil Schürer, *The History of the Jewish People in the Age of Jesus Christ (Volume 2)*, rev. and ed. Geza Vermes, Fergus Millar, and Matthew Black <Edinburgh: T. & T. Clark, 1979>, p. 465).

[16] "The exile was proof that the covenantal relationship was broken, and with it the legitimate claim to the land" (John Van Seters, *Abraham in History and Tradition* <New Haven: Yale University Press, 1975>, p. 265).

nations that destroyed Israel and annihilated Jerusalem's Jewish population.[17] The Bible, too, emphasized that they were unbelievers. For the Bible and for the poet-composer of the Psalms of Solomon, it was irrelevant whether the destroyer of God's people believed in God or not. God can and did raise up unbelievers to kill God's people.

The poet-composer of the Psalms of Solomon lays this down as an important principle for the Late Second Temple Period; God uses unbelievers and non-believing nations to completely destroy God's people and this is a normative way God operates in the world. This must be seen as a warning by the poet-composer of the Psalms of Solomon to the Hasmoneans. The Hasmoneans must not exult in their victory over the Syrians and think that God will protect them regardless of what they do. God can and will raise up unbelievers to destroy them and the Jerusalem Temple that they have usurped from the hands of the legitimate Zadokite priests. The blatant emphasis on the unbelieving nature of the foreign destroyer of the Jerusalem Temple and Israel should be seen as a veiled threat to the Hasomeans by the Zadokite poet-compoer who wrote his Psalms of Solomon as pro-Zadokite propaganda.

Psalms of Solomon 17:16 continues the emphasis that the conquering Gentile ruler was an unbeliever. The poet-composer describes the foreign ruler occupying Jerusalem, and this foreign ruler did what foreign rulers do in their cities to their gods. In other words, King Nebuchadnezzar worshipped his gods in the city of Jerusalem. After his occupation, the city of Jerusalem was thoroughly turned into a city that worshipped foreign gods. This fact is stated to emphasize that King Nebuchadnezzar was in no way a believer of God. The important message, or course, is that God raised up an unbeliever to destroy a believing nation and the chosen people of God.

Psalms of Solomon 17:17-22 describes why such things happened in Jerusalem. In a sense, verses 17-22 can be seen as a historical accounting of the causes for why God brought in a truly foreign unbeliever to destroy the chosen people of God and the chosen city of God. Psalms of Solomon 17:17 describes that the children of the covenant surpassed the Gentiles in doing evil.[18] This is

---

[17] Bilha Nitzan writes regarding the Zadokite perspective found in Qumran: "Thus, according to the concept of holiness held by the *Yahad*, so long as the purity of the Temple was not properly kept, Israel was left in the same dangerous situation as when the polluted sanctuary had been left by God to its doom when it was destroyed physically in 586 B.C.E." (Bilha Nitzan, "The Idea of Holiness in Qumran Poetry and Liturgy" in *Sapiential, Liturgical and Poetic Texts from Qumran: Proceedings of the Third Meeting of the International Organization for Qumran Studies, Oslo 1998*, ed. Daniel K. Falk, Florentino García Martínez, and Eileen Schuller <Leiden: Brill, 2000, pp. 127-145>, p. 130).

[18] "Yahweh's choice of Israel, therefore, is contingent – both in the sense that history moves on, and that all depend on Israel's faithfulness to the covenant. . . . The election of Israel does not lose sight of other places (nations) or other times. The land which

consistent with the accusations found in the Old Testament against the Israelites. Prophetic book after prophetic book accuses Israelites of transgressing God's law worse than the unbelieving nations around them, and this was the reason why God has chosen to destroy Israel and decimate the Jews. In other words, the Jews were not only covenant breakers, they were more evil than unbelievers so that they deserved the judgment that went their way. The poet-composer of Psalms of Solomon 17:17 specifically points out two transgressions; namely, not pursuing mercy and truth. In fact, verse 17 argues that there was not a single person who pursued mercy and truth. It was important for the poet-composer to argue that there was no one righteous to argue that God was completely righteous in completely decimating Jerusalem's population and destroying Israel. And the two transgressions specifically mentioned are reminiscent of the transgressions emphasized by Old Testament prophets. Amos and Hosea emphasized that not pursuing mercy–or a fair justice system that does not oppress the poor, such as widows and orphans, and give power to the wealthy – and truth – that is, the Word of God as the rule for political rule and governance of the country's people – were the causes for which God decided to completely destroy the country. The poet-composer of the Psalms of Solomon specifically mentions Jerusalem as the place in which there was absence of those pursuing mercy and truth. The understanding, of course, is that it was appropriate that God sent in a foreign, unbelieving ruler and his army to completely destroy Jerusalem and decimate the Jewish population.

Psalms of Solomon 17:18 continues with the emphasis that Jerusalem was thoroughly evil. It was because Jerusalem was so evil that the righteous people fled from Jerusalem. In a sense, verse 18 highlights the irony that righteous people have to flee Jerusalem. In fact, verse 18 emphasizes that those who loved the assembly of the saints fled from Jerusalem. The irony, of course, is that the Jerusalem Temple was in Jerusalem, and it was thought that the saints would necessarily be in Jerusalem at the holy assemblies of the Jerusalem Temple. But this belittling of the cultic ceremonies of the Jerusalem Temple by the poet-composer of the Psalms of Solomon is consistent with his thematic concern that proper cultic worship be carried out in the Jerusalem Temple. If proper cultic worship is not carried out in the Jerusalem Temple, then the Jerusalem Temple becomes unnecessarily at least in the sight of God; in other words, the Jerusalem Temple must have proper cultic worship to retain its redemptive value. This explains why the righteous people who crave the assembly of the saints fled from Jerusalem even as the Jerusalem Temple stood. And this explains the

---

becomes Israel's inheritance will be held in a certain tension arising from this. It may, indeed will, be lost–but may also be regained. Thus, in relation to his immanent (covenantal) presence in the world, Yahweh retains his freedom–a function of his transcendence" (J. G. McConville, "Time, Place, and the Deueronomic Altar-Law," in *Time and Place in Deuteronomy*, ed. J. G. McConville and J. G. Millar <Sheffield: Sheffield Academic Press, 1994, pp. 89-139>, pp. 136-137).

reason why God destroyed the Jerusalem Temple in the days of King Nebuchadnezzar.

Psalms of Solomon 17:18's emphasis on proper cultic worship in the Jerusalem Temple as giving it a redemptive value must be seen, at least in part, as the poet-composer's proactive support of the Zadokites who scattered away from Jerusalem. The Zadokite poet-composer of the Psalms of Solomon was interested in defending why the Zadokites went off into Leontopolis, Egypt, while the Jerusalem Temple stood. He is interested in engaging in pro-Zadokite propaganda to justify the fact that a group of Zadokites and their supporters went off to the Judean Desert to establish an ascetic community in Qumran.[19] What they did was not wrong because the Jerusalem Temple with its illegitimate Hasmonean priests have defiled the Jerusalem Temple's proper cultic worship.

Psalms of Solomon 17:19 clearly shows that the poet-composer of the Psalms of Solomon is defending the Zadokites who have fled Jerusalem. This is particularly interesting because the poet-composer of the Psalms of Solomon seems to go off in a long-winded digression with verse 19. This is understandable in light of the fact that the poet-composer of the Psalms of Solomon was himself a Zadokite, and it was personal for him that the Zadokites were scattered and made to wander through deserts in search of safety. Of course, on the surface-level reading of this text, the poet-composer of the Psalms of Solomon is describing the scattering of the righteous at the time of the end of the First Temple Period. The poet-composer is writing that towards the end of the First Temple Period, Jerusalem had become thoroughly evil and there was no holy assembly there acceptable to God. This surface recounting of the last days of the First Temple is congruent with the account given in the Old Testament. But of course, beyond the surface reading is a deep concern of the poet-composer with the current state of Zadokites scattered all over away from Jerusalem. Thus, Psalms of Solomon 17:19-22 should be seen as a personal digression that belie the deeply personal pain felt by the Zadokite poet-composer about the Hasmoneans who have usurped the Jerusalem Temple and the Jewish people who followed them.

Psalms of Solomon 17:19 describes how many Zadokites were scattered away from Jerusalem. Not only was it a departure to seek holiness and to protest Jerusalem's wayward nature, it was also a flight born out of necessity. The Zadokites were, in fact, fleeing for their lives. The Hasmoneans who had usurped the Jerusalem Temple were seeking to kill many Zadokites who posed a threat to their hegemony and political influence in the capital city. There were understandably purges and threats of purges ubiquitous for Zadokites in and

---

[19] Lawrence H. Schiffman writes: "To them an illegitimate shrine was the same as a nonexistent shrine" (Lawrence H. Schiffman, "The Dead Sea Scrolls and Rabbinic Halakhah" in *The Dead Sea Scrolls as Background to Postbiblical Judaism and Early Christianity: Papers from an International Conference at St. Andrews in 2001*, ed. James R. Davila <Leiden: Brill, 2003, pp. 3-24>, p. 18).

near Jerusalem. This account is consistent with the testimony of the Qumran documents. There was the Wicked Priest in Jerusalem who sought to destroy the Sons of Zadok. Zadokite priest had to flee to save their lives. In fact, many Zadokite priests were killed by the Wicked Priest who had assumed power in the Jerusalem Temple. The wicked Hasmonean priest who usurped the office of the High Priest of the Jerusalem Temple was interested in consolidating his power through purges of Zadokites and their supporters. Thus, Zadokite priests fled Jerusalem and many wandered through the dessert in search of safety. Psalms of Solomon 17:19 describes one life that was saved that was particularly precious. Of course, this is pointing to the Teacher of Righteousness, who settled in Qumran with his supporters and followers. Verse 19 clearly shows that the Zadokite poet-composer placed his sympathies with the Teacher of Righteousness in Qumran. He saw him as a precious, righteous person who was made to flee from the Wicked Priest, the Hasmonean priest who had usurped the office of the High Priest at the Jerusalem Temple.

Psalms of Solomon 17:20 continues on a digressive note. Of course, the surface reading is meant to be placed in the context of the last days of the First Temple Period, but the digression belies the Zadokite poet-composer's concern with the present day. Having inferred to the Teacher of Righteousness, a precious Zadokite priest who had saved himself in the desert, the Zadokite poet-composer describes the plight of other Zadokites.[20] They were pursued by the Hasmoneans and their supporters so that they scattered all over the earth. Since the poet-composer was Zadokite himself, he knew what was going on with his family and friends who were Zadokites. Such personal knowledge would have evaded non-Zadokites in Israel. In fact, many non-Zadokites would not have concerned themselves with the plight of the Zadokites. They were concerned about celebrating the Jewish rule of Jerusalem, and many were happy to submit themselves under the rule of the Hasmoneans, who they perceived freed them from Syrian bondage. The concern of the Zadokites was least in their minds. Of course, things were different among the Zadokites themselves who experienced adversity with the change in power and political dynamics in Jerusalem. It is with this plight of the fellow Zadokites that the poet-composer of the Psalms of Solomon identifies.

Psalms of Solomon 17:21 uses poetic language to explain God's divine displeasure at what was going on. God engaged in nature manipulation to

---

[20] Daniel R. Schwartz writes: "This last point brings us back to Qumran: May we not assume that emphasis on submission to Zadokite priests in the literature of this sect that emerged in the early Hasmonean period testifies that it, too, opposed the Hasmonean high priests because they lacked the proper, Zadokite, descent?" (Daniel R. Schwartz, "On Two Aspects of Priestly Descent at Qumran" in *Archaeology and History in the Dead Sea Scrolls: The New York University Conference in Memory of Yigael Yadin*, ed. Lawrence H. Schiffman <Sheffield: Sheffield Academic Press, 1990, pp. 157-179>, p. 165).

exhibit his divine judgment; God stayed the fountains. The Old Testament shows that one way that God judged the Israelites for their cultic violations was through a draught. Lack of water brought lack of food, and there was famine throughout the land. This is what actually happened during the last days of the First Temple Period, as the Old Testament shows. Of course, like the digressions in the previous verses, the Zadokite poet-composer was interested in focusing on the situation of the Zadokites of his day. Thus, he is keenly interested in showing that the judgement of God was applicable to the Jews of his day. The problem, of course, was that there was no draught during his time. In fact, the only draught that could be talked about is the draught in the dessert where the Zadokites and their supporters were wandering to protect their life. Thus, it is not surprising that the Zadokite poet-composer spritualizes the draught, or the staying of the fountain. He does this by describing the fountains that were stayed; the fountains were everlasting fountains. Of course, there are no everlasting fountains on earth; all streams of earthly waters are finite. Thus, when the term of everlasting fountains is used, it must be recognized that this was referring to spiritual blessing or life. The fact that the everlasting fountain is referring to spiritual blessing or life can be understood from the imagery that the poet-composer utilizes; he states that these everlasting fountains spring out of the depths and from high mountains. And depths are places where God is often described to reside; often, the depths are used as metaphor for God Himself. In a sense, therefore, God Himself blocked the everlasting spiritual blessing because of the current situation. Also, high mountains point to places of worship. There were high places of worship in Jerusalem and competing holy mountains. Mount Moriah is where the Jerusalem Temple was believed to have stood, but there was a holy high place in Shiloh as well. The poet-composer is, in effect, stating that all the high places in Israel were now blocked from being sources of spiritual blessing and life because of what was done to the Zadokites; they were made to wander through the desert to protect their lives from the usurpers of holy places of God in Israel. The Zadokite poet-composer is careful to lay the blame on the current political and religious leadership of Jerusalem and their supporters. The poet-composer states in Psalms of Solomon 17:21: "From their ruler to the vilest of the people, they were altogether sinful."[21] The ruler was sinful because he had usurped the legitimate position of the Zadokites, and the people were sinful because they had gone along with the wishes of the unrighteous ruler.

Psalms of Solomon 17:22, which concludes the historical portion–and particularly the digressive part within it–reiterates the evil of the whole populace of Jerusalem which went along with the disenfranchisement and persecution of the Zadokites. The poet-composer writes: "The king was a transgressor, and the judge was disobedient, and the people sinful." It is important to remember that

---

[21] Cf. 1QpHab 12; CD 1:3-13.

the Hasmonean High Priest of the Jerusalem Temple has made himself king over Israel. In a sense, the Hasmonean High Priest committed two transgressions; namely, he usurped the position of the high priest belonging to Zadokites and he took on a title of king. Thus, the king–or the Hasmonean High Priest who declared himself the king–was a transgressor of God's cultic law. The judge was disobedient because he was disobedient to God. The judge should have upheld the Law of God and made sure that cultic laws were not violated. But this did not happen, obviously, since the Hasmoneans usurped key cultic offices. And the people were sinful because they went along with all the transgression against God's cultic laws. Thus, everyone in Jerusalem was culpable and deserving of divine punishment. In a sense, the verse concluding the historical portion shows the situation of the last days of the First Temple Period and the current state of the Hasmonean dynasty as being analogous. Thus, the Zadokite poet-composer presents a veiled threat to his readership.

It is not surprising, therefore, that the historical portion is followed by the apocalyptic portion, encased in Psalms of Solomon 17:23-51. Just like the historical and apologetic portions, this apocalyptic section is pro-Zadokite propaganda. The main way this pro-Zadokite propaganda is achieved is through privileging of a Davidic messianic figure. Since King David and his line represented the royalty legitimating the Zadokites as the most important priestly line to occupy the office of the High Priest of the Jerusalem Temple, it is not surprising that any pro-Zadokite propaganda will involve an aggressive pro-Davidic ideology. In other words, an emphatic pro-Davidic messianism can be seen as pro-Zadokite. In a way, therefore, am emphasis on a Davidic messiah can be seen as anti-Hasmonean in essence. Thus, the Hasmoneans and their supporters were adverse to a strong Davidic messianism. This explains why Qumran had a strong Davidic messianism. Qumran envisioned a double-messiahship: a military messiah of the Davidic line and a priestly messiah of the line of Aaron. Of course, the Aaronic messiah would be Zadokite. Even in places where the Qumran community emphasized a sole messiah, it emphasized a messiah of the Davidic line. In such cases, of course, it is understood the High Priest serving in the Jerusalem Temple under a Davidic king would be Zadokite. Whether explicitly mentioned or not, a strong Davidic messianism necessarily was pro-Zadokite in nature. This was the case in Qumran, and this was the case in Jerusalem. The poet-composer of the Psalms of Solomon was a Zadokite who wanted to emphasize a pro-Davidic messianism in support of a Zadokite priestly line dominating in the Jerusalem Temple. This explains the pro-Zadokite propaganda encased in aggressive Davidic messianism of Psalms of Solomon 17:23-51.

The pro-Davidic messianism of Psalms of Solomon 17:23-51 is described in apocalyptic terms. Verse 23 emphasizes that a Davidic king is the norm. This is certainly an insult to the Hasmoneans who had usurped the office of the High Priest as well as King. Not only were the Hasmoneans not of the line of David so that they were illegitimate royals, but they were also not Zadokites, a legitimately priestly line instituted by the Davidic throne. The emphasis on the Davidic king must be seen as intentionally pro-Zadokite in tone. Furthermore, this intentional pro-Davidic stance gains ideological momentum in the call for the LORD to install a rightful Davidic king. Of course, the idea is that it has always been the intention of the LORD God Himself that a Davidic king rules in Jerusalem, so the fact that a non-Davidic king was ruling in Jerusalem was incompatible with the desire of God, and, therefore, it was opposed to God's covenantal plan itself. The poet-composer of the Psalms of Solomon further emphasizes that still it is a part of the on-going providential work of God since it is God who desires to install a rightful Davidic king to the throne of Israel at a future time. Certainly, this is an intentional slight at the Hasmoneans of Jerusalem who had kicked out the Zadokites. The Hasmonean reign in Jerusalem was not only illegitimate but opposed to God's plan for Israel. And God will put into motion His plan for a Davidic king in His own time. Of course, this would be in His apocalyptic time.

The strong apocalyptic nature is emphasized in the next following verses. In Psalms of Solomon 17:24, the Zadokite poet-composer emphasizes that God will give strength to the Davidic messianic figure so that he could "break in pieces them that rule unjustly." It is evident that this apocalyptic language is directed against the Hasmonean rulers of Jerusalem in the time that the poet-composer wrote the Psalms of Solomon. The Hasmonean king was ruling unjustly especially in regards to how he treated the Zadokites. The Hasmonean dynasty has driven out the Zadokites from Jerusalem. In fact, the very fact that the Hasmoneans ruled in Jerusalem and occupied the Jerusalem Temple represented an unjust rule that had to be overthrown.

The apocalyptic tone of Psalms of Solomon 17:24 is continued in the next verse; verse 25 calls for the purging of Jerusalem of Gentiles who trample down on Jerusalem to destroy it. To be sure, there were Gentiles in Jerusalem during the days of the Hasmoneans. Many of these Gentiles lived in Jerusalem, and some of them intermarried with Jews in Jerusalem. Whether they intermarried or not, these Gentiles influenced the character of the city of Jerusalem and contributed to its Hellenized nature. In fact, the Gentiles cannot be solely to blame. Jerusalem as a city was thoroughly Hellenized. Contrary to popular misconception, the Maccabean Revolt was not necessarily anti-Gentile. In fact, the sole purpose of the Maccabean Revolt was to drive out Antiochus IV Epiphanes from Jerusalem because he had defiled the Jerusalem Temple and was offering pagan sacrifices in it. The Maccabean Revolt should be seen, therefore, more as a nationalist movement for political independence, rather than an ideological war or even a religious war. The real issue for Jews who fought the Syrians was the right to rule their own land, or political independence. In essence, therefore, the Maccabean Revolt can be seen as a struggle for self-determination. Of course, there were Jews who were upset that they were forbidden to keep kosher, to observe Sabbath days, and be circumcised. However, it must be noted that Jerusalem was thoroughly Hellenized at the time of the Maccabean Revolt. Thus, it is even conceivable that the majority of the Jewish population in Jerusalem were not rigid about observing Jewish traditions, such as circumcision, a strictly kosher diet, and Sabbath day observance. To be sure, even many Hellenized Jews who did not keep these customs valued the Jerusalem Temple as a redemptive medium for the Jewish people.

To be Jewish meant to acknowledge the centrality of the Jerusalem Temple for Jewish identity. But other identity markers, such as circumcision, a kosher diet, and Sabbath day observance were not necessarily agreed upon identity marker for those who considered themselves as Jews as the Jerusalem Temple was. It was impossible to call oneself Jewish if he did not value the Jerusalem Temple. But in other regulations, the rules were more relaxed. Many Jewish sects disagreed with each other. This is clear because during the Hasmonean times, there was great dissent in belief and practices between various Jewish sects, such as the Pharisees and the Sadducees. The Pharisees emphasized kosher and Sabbath day laws, but the Sadducees did not; certainly, the Sadducees were not rigid about them. Thus, to presume that the Maccabean Revolt and the rededication of the Jerusalem Temple by the Hasmoneans represented a thorough reform of all Jerusalem would be historically inaccurate. Those who were Hellenized before the Maccabean Revolt continued to be Hellenized after the success of the revolt. Those who were strictly observant of kosher and Sabbath day laws before the Maccabean Revolt were observant after the success of the Maccabean Revolt. There was, to be sure, movement between the strictly observant camp and the completely non-observant camp; some became observant who were previously not observant and vice versa. And there was a large grey zone in the middle where some tried to keep kosher but did not strictly keep Sabbath day laws. Some maintained Sabbath day regulations but did not abide by kosher laws. Some were relaxed about both Sabbath day and kosher laws but tried to keep them whenever possible. The issue of the Maccabean Revolt was not over legal observance but over political independence and the preservation of the Jerusalem Temple, the primary and perhaps the sole unifying symbol of importance for all Jews regardless of their particular religious-observance preference. Thus, it cannot be denied that Jerusalem before the Maccabean Revolt was thoroughly Hellenized and Jerusalem after the Maccabean Revolt was thoroughly Hellenized as well. In fact, Jerusalem under the Hasmoneans became more aggressively Hellenized. The pro-Hellenistic proclivity of the Hasmoneans is clear in their names. Although they ruled over a Jewish kingdom, they took for themselves Greek names. This showed that they preferred Greek ways to Hebrew ways; they preferred Greek traditions to Hebrew traditions. Of course for those who were strictly observant, the aggressively pro-Hellenistic leanings of the Hasmoneans were anathema.[22]

The Qumran community, which was a rigidly observing Jewish community, would have particularly been offended by the pro-Hellenistic leanings of the Hasmoneans. As it were, the Qumran community was a Zadokite community—or more correctly, a reformist Zadokite community. Thus, these Zadokites at Qumran and their supporters considered Jerusalem under the Hasmoneans to be under the interdict of God. The Jerusalem Temple was defiled merely by the presence of the Hasmoneans in its leadership. And the Qumranites awaited the Day of Judgement, an apocalyptic end to the current leadership in Jerusalem. Although not as aggressively blatant as they nor desiring for isolation, the Zadokite poet-composer of the Psalms of Solomon was a sympathizer, who essentially believed that the Zadokites at Qumran were the righteous remnant who should be restored to rule in Jerusalem. It was the success of the apocalyptic judgement that would purge the Jerusalem of its Gentile ways. As long as the Hasmoneans ruled in Jerusalem, Jerusalem would be rampant with Gentiles and Gentile ways. The poet-composer of the Psalms of Solomon thought that there was something seriously wrong with an independent Jewish state where the rulers preferred Gentiles and their traditions over Jewish traditions and Jewish ways.

Psalms of Solomon 17:26 shows that the target of the Zadokite poet-composer's venom was directed primarily at the Hasmoneans, whom he calls "sinners." The sinners, obviously contrasted with the Gentiles, represented Jews who refused to observe Jewish cultic regulations and the Law of Moses. Psalms of Solomon 17:26 clearly shows that "sinners" in the verse refers to Jews who violate covenantal requirements and cultic regulations since the poet-composer of the Psalms of Solomon threatens that these sinners will be thrust out from their inheritance. The inheritance referred to here is the inheritance according to God's covenant. Only those under the covenant had a right to the inheritance under the covenant, and only they could be thrown out from the covenant that was their right insofar as they observed the covenant. The apocalyptic threat in this context, of course, refers to the expelling of the Hasmoneans from Jerusalem and restoring of Jerusalem to the legitimate high priest of Jerusalem, the Zadokites. Not only will these "sinners" be denied their right to enjoy covenantal blessing in the Land of the Promise, these "sinners" will have their proud spirits destroyed. This can be seen as a threat to the lives of Hasmoneans in the apocalyptic judgment. The apocalyptic threat of verse 26 is again rephrased in prophetic imagery reminiscent of the prophetic book of Amos

---

[22] Martin Hengel states regarding the Qumran community: "It therefore can be understood, *inter alia*, as a movement of strict opposition against the expansion of Hellenistic civilization in Jewish Palestine" (Martin Hengel, "Qumran and Hellenism" in *Religion in the Dead Sea Scrolls*, ed. John J. Collins and Robert A. Kugler <Grand Rapids: William B. Eerdmans Publishing Company, 2000, pp. 46-56>, p. 46).

regarding the coming Day of the LORD: "As potter's vessels with a rod of iron shall he break in pieces all their substance." It is clear why the poet-composer of the Psalms of Solomon uses language reminiscent of the prophetic language of the Old Testament. In the Old Testament, the prophets of God spoke against the Israelites and threatened them with destruction. The fact that the Israelites were the children of the promise and a covenant-partner of God did not prevent God from utterly destroying them. In the same manner, God can and will destroy the Jews of the poet-composer's day. In a sense, the Zadokite poet-composer is establishing the possibility for God's destruction of the Hasmoneans. The prophetic language and imagery not only depict the image of God's thorough judgement, it also shows the apocalyptic language to be consistent with the Holy Scriptures.

Psalms of Solomon 17:27 continues the apocalyptic language of judgment. But at initial reading, this verse seems to be about the judgment of foreign nations rather than of the Hasmoneans and of Jerusalem. Upon closer examination, however, it is plain to see that the focus of the judgment is on the Hasmoneans. Verse 27 starts out with the proclamation that the Davidic messianic figure will destroy the nations with the words of his mouth. Although at first this is focusing on the upcoming destructions of Gentile nations, what comes right after this proclamation shows that even the seeming apocalyptic end of the foreign nations is meant as a judgment of the sinners in Jerusalem; namely, the Hasmoneans. When the Davidic messiah drives away the Gentile nations through his rebuke, the result will be that the "sinners" in Jerusalem will be convicted in the thoughts of their heart. Thus, the Zadokite poet-composer of the Psalms of Solomon shows the reason for the driving away of the Gentile nations; it is to convict the Hasmoneans in Jerusalem. This cause-and-effect is understandable in light of the fact that the Hasmoneans in Jerusalem were thoroughly Hellenized. Not only did they personally prefer Hellenized ways and associated with Hellenized Gentiles, thereby filling Jerusalem with Hellenistic individuals and influence, they actually made alliances with the nations around them that gave them political and military power. In a sense, the Hasmonean dynasty derived their power in large part through their courting of foreign and Gentile nations to prop up their authority and influence. When God's appointed Davidic messiah arrives on the scene during apocalyptic days and drive away the foreign Gentile nations, he will in effect undermine the power base of the Hasmoneans. In this light, it is easy to understand why driving away the Gentile nations is a way to convict the Hasmoneans; it exposes their weakness as their power base tied to Hellenistic powers is worn away. In this regard, it is significant that the conviction of the sinners is on the thoughts of their heart. Obviously, this is a condemnation of the Hellenistic proclivities of the Hasmonean dynasty. The Hasmoneans may be the high priests of the Jerusalem Temple, and they may be the political leaders of the so-called Jewish state, but in reality, the Hasmoneans did not have a heart that was pleasing to the LORD.

Their hearts were thoroughly Hellenized and secularized. The Hasmonean priests may have conducted Jerusalem Temple cultic rituals out of form, but they were not sincerely submitting to the cultic rules in their heart. The Zadokite poet-composer thus brought a charge against the Hasmonean priests whose outward ceremonies and cultic leadership concealed their rampant Hellenstic heart and mind.

Psalms of Solomon 17:28 continues to engage in anti-Hasmonean and pro-Zadokite propaganda by using apocalyptic language. In verse 28, the Zadokite poet-composer states that the Davidic messiah will gather together to himself a holy people, whom he will lead in righteousness. This is meant as a direct attack on the Hasmoneans. Basically, the Zadokite poet-composer is accusing the Hasmoneans of two things. First, the Hasmoneans fail to gather together a holy people. In this accusation, the Zadokite poet-composer is charging the Hasmoneans of gathering together an unholy people. There was no question that there were a lot of Jews in Jerusalem and that many of them were followers of the Hasmoneans. Of course, the Hasmoneans surrounded themselves with those Jews who were aggressively pro-Hasmonean and anti-Zadokite. They were, in fact, careful to drive out the Zadokites from Jerusalem either through pro-active persecution and attack or by making them feel as uncomfortable as possible in their stay in Jerusalem. Hasmoneans were effective in surrounding themselves with Jews, but these Jews were, in the accusation of the Zadokite poet-composer, unholy people. In contrast to self-seeking Hasmoneans, the Davidic messiah will surround himself with holy people, such as the holy Zadokites and their strictly observant supporters in Qumran. The second charge of the Zadokie poet-composer against the Hasmoneans is that they do not lead in righteousness. There may have been many reasons for such an accusation. Of course, the most egregious unrighteousness in their leadership was the proliferating of Gentile influence and Hellenistic value system and the driving out of the Zadokites. When Jerusalem is restored to a rightful Davidic ruler in apocalyptic days, it will be led by righteous leaders who will gather a holy assembly and lead with righteousness according to proper cultic observance.

The latter part of verse 28 emphasizes that this apocalyptic Davidic king will judge the tribes of the people that has been sanctified by his God. It should be noted that this second part of Psalms of Solomon 17:28 is strategically pro-Zadokite and anti-Hasmonean as well. It is pro-Zadokite to emphasize the tribes of Israel. Why is this a strategy of pro-Zadokite propaganda? It is important to note that the legitimacy of the Zadokites to lead the Jerusalem Temple is based on blood lineage to Zadok. Thus, it was important for pro-Zadokites to emphasize actual lineage as very important. Of course, the Hasmoneans were interested in downplaying actual lineage and emphasizing a type of spiritual link because they lacked the actual lineage to the legitimate high priestly line. The use of the language of the tribes of Israel is meant to remind the reader that there is a legitimate line of high priests and they are the Zadokites. These Zadokites have been displaced from Jerusalem, and that was not right. It can be seen as a type of a call for restoration of the dispersed Zadokites to Jerusalem. The Zadokite poet-composer believed that the apocalyptic end will gather together the legitimate Zadokites to Jerusalem to lead sanctified assemblies. It is important to note, of course, that the call for a Davidic messiah was an emphasis on actual blood lineage to King David in the same way as the Zadokites claimed their legitimacy based on their blood lineage to Zadok.

Psalms of Solomon 17:29 continues in pro-Zadokite propaganda by separating the Zadokites and the Davidic line from the rest of the Jews. The line of Zadok was special and so was the line of King David. None of the Jews who were not descended directly in this line could be seen as being on the same level with them. This, of course, was an insult to the Hasmoneans who did not have any special blood lineage to set them apart in a really particular way. In fact, the Hasmoneans arose from among the midst of "regular" Jews. Thus, Psalms of Solomon 17:29 emphasizes that the messianic king of Davidic line – and of course by extension, the Sons of Zadok–would not set apart from the masses. The Zadokite poet-composer gives the reason for their separation as their holiness. Psalms of Solomon 17:29 states that no one who is unholy can dwell with them.

Psalms of Solomon 17:30 continues in the vein of emphasizing the special quality of the Davidic messiah and by analogy the Zadokite priests in that the Zadokite poet-composer entrusts them with the responsibility of portioning Israel according to each tribe. Verse 30 actually specifically points to the Davidic messiah as dividing the land according to each tribe, but it is implied and understood that those who would carry out the work of dividing the land according to each tribe would be entrusted to the priests of the Davidic messiah, or the Zadokites. This is clear in the emphasis in Psalms of Solomon 17:30 that the messianic king of Davidic line would ascertan that they would be sons of their God. In other words, the Davidic messiah would ascertan their worthiness as the children of the covenant. How would this be ascertained? Of course, the military messiah of Davidic line would not be engaging in the assessment himself; rather, he would employ his priests, the Zadokites. Zadokites as priests who are concerned with ritual purity, cultic observance, and faithfulness to the covenant will be the ones who will ascertain who the true sons of God are. And those who are deemed to be true sons of God will be given land according to their tribe. It is important to recognize that granting of such great powers to the Davidic messiah was tantamount to imbuing the Zadokites with maximum priestly powers; after all, Zadokites were the priests legitimated by the Davidic line.

Psalms of Solomon 17:30 is significant in its explicit emphasis of the tribes of Israel. Verse 30 emphasizes that once the true "sons of God" are determined, they will be allotted land according to their tribes. This is important for two reasons. First of all, this is significant because the emphasis on lineage – which tribal connections certainly are—highlights the emphasis on lineage of the priests. And of course, the emphasis on priestly lineage is meant to stress the idea that the Zadokites were the legitimate priests to inhabit the office of the high priests. Their lineage itself is the determining factor. Thus, hereditary origin of individuals is emphasized, and it is this emphasis that gives away the aggressively pro-Zadokite nature of the Psalms of Solomon and the Zadokite identity of its author. Secondly, the emphasis on the tribe harkens back to the covenant of God. God promised Abraham the land and it was given to his descendants. This land, which was given to Abraham's descendants after the Conquest of Joshua, was divided up according to tribes. In a sense, land division according to tribes was seen as the ultimate fruition of the promise made by God to Abraham of the possession of the land. Thus, by describing the tribal division of land, the poet-author of the Psalms of Solomon was trying to remind his Jewish readers that blood lineage was important. Of course, there was a clear ulterior motive in this emphasis.

Since the Hasmoneans were not of the blood-lineage of the Zadokites, emphasizing the importance of the blood-lineage was a way to argue for Zadokite priesthood occupying Jerusalem Temple leadership positions. The propagandistic nature of the stress on the division of the land by tribe is highlighted in the fact that most of the Jews of the Late Second Temple Period did not know which tribe they belonged to. Furthermore, most of the ordinary people in the street could not verify their tribal connections even if they may have claimed to be from a particular tribe. It is important to remember the Exile—it was long and it scattered everybody in every directions. It was hard to keep track of particular tribe association because various tribes lived among each other, and they often mixed. The cohabitation diluted stress on tribal associations. More importantly, Jews lived among Gentiles in Gentile lands, and their tribal associations basically became irrelevant. For many Jews, it was important just to survive in Gentile lands, so many Jews did not fuss about their particular tribal identity. In fact, many Jews married Gentiles. This is clear from the book of Esther, where marrying a Gentile is not seen as a problem at all. Furthermore, pervasive intermarriage between Jews and Gentiles is clearly documented in Nehemiah's call to Jews to divorce their Gentile wives. Of course, Nehemiah's order was the ideal, but it is important to know that the ideal of the pure Jewish family was not feasible in many cases. It can be assumed that the program of divorcing Gentiles idealized and pushed for by Nehemiah and the leaders of the Return to Zion were not practiced by ordinary Jews. Jewish father with a Gentile wife and five children was not likely to divorce his Gentile wife, who cooked for him and took care of the kids, even if he no longer actually loved her. It should be assumed that many Jews remained married to Gentiles, and there were some Gentiles who were hostile toward the Jewish religion. This, of course, would have diluted Jewish religious identity at home, including that of the Jewish husband. But that was the reality of the time of the rebuilding of the Second Temple. This partly explains the rampant Hellenization among the "Jewish" populace in Palestine in the Late Second Temple Period, including those who were supposedly orthodox. In fact, in many ways, normative "Jewish" culture in Palestine was Hellenistic and not identifiable with Hebrew culture. This is not surprising given that Jews lived generations in the Exile. If one examines Jewish families in America, England, Brazil, and Bulgaria, one can note that their family culture is quite identical with the larger culture around them. This makes a lot of sense since they have lived many generations in that land. There was no such thing as "Jewish" culture; being Jewish was a religion. And even this Jewish religious identity was diluted by intermarriage with members of other religions or those who essentially held to no religion. Thus, when the Zadokite poet-composer emphasized tribal lineage, it was meant to be a key signifier[23] to recall the collective memory of the covenant and its fulfilment in the division of the Promised Land according to tribes and to prompt the Jewish listeners to action in supporting the Zadokites instead of the Hasmoneans who were enthroned in power positions of the Jerusalem Temple.

Psalms of Solomon 17:32-35 continues in the direction of pro-Zadokite propaganda. These verses do so via the emphasis on the purification of Jerusalem by the hand of a Davidic messiah. Obviously, when a Davidic king purges Jerusalem, he will use his Zadokite priests to do so. So, it is easy to see why the emphasis on a Davidic messiah is necessarily tied to emphasizing that a Zadokite must be the High Priest at the Jerusalem Temple. Psalms of Solomon 17:33 stresses that the Davidic king will purge the Jerusalem Temple and make it holy like in the days of old. Of course, the accusation is that the current Jerusalem Temple is not very holy. Things are not right with the world; Hasmoneans have usurped the rightful office of the Zadokite priests. The current chaos embodied in the displacement of the Zadokite priests–disruption in the orderly world as dictated by God since the days of King David–requires an apocalyptic judgment which the Davidic messiah will bring about. And it will be through this apocalyptic war that *tikkun olam* (reordering of the broken world) will be brought about. Although the Zadokite poet-composer does not explicitly mention it, the apocalyptic war waged by the Davidic messiah will not only be against the Gentiles but also against the Jews in Jerusalem; in other words, the Davidic messiah will destroy both Gentiles and Jews.

The Hasmoneans and their followers have unlawfully (in light of the laws pertaining to the appropriate persons to occupy the office of the High Priest of the Jerusalem Temple) taken control of Jerusalem and their very presence in the Jerusalem Temple defiles the Jerusalem Temple and corrupts cultic worship. This Zadokite line of thinking is commonly found among other pro-Zadokite writings. In fact, writings from Qumran assume that the Davidic messiah will

---

[23] See Heerak Christian Kim, *Key Signifier as Literary Device: Its Definition and Function in Literature and Media* (Lewiston: The Edwin Mellen Press, 2006).

purge Jerusalem of Jews; in other words, the Davidic messiah will kill Jews in Jerusalem to purify the Jerusalem Temple. The Jew-on-Jew violence espoused fundamentally by the Qumranites and supported by the Zadokite poet-composer of the Psalms of Solomon may not agree with Solomon Schlecther's Zionist vision for the unity of the Jewish people regardless of their particular leanings religiously within the wide scope of Judaism, but it was a very real and even central tenet of the Zadokites of the Late Second Temple Period. But it would be unfair to assume that the Zadokites espoused killing of fellow Jews merely for the restoration of their position lost in Jerusalem; many probably truly believed that the Zadokite priesthood was the rightful priests for the office of the High Priest of the Jerusalem Temple. Tradition and history confirmed this.

Furthermore, it would be historically wrong to assume that the Zadokites were the only ones who supported Jew-on-Jew violence. In fact, Jews killing Jews was not seen as abnormal; there are not writings from the Late Second Temple Period fundamentally barring Jews from killing other Jews. In fact, the Late Second Temple Period can be seen as a period of perpetual conflict between Jews. Jews killed Jews in the Late Second Temple Period. Some of the mass killings were recorded, and others were not recorded. The crucifixion of the Pharisees by the Hasmoneans was recorded by Josephus, but he does not record the violent conflict between the Zadokites and the Hasmoneans. Before the discovery of the Dead Sea Scrolls, many scholars of Jewish history doubted the aggressively violent nature of the conflict between the Hasmoneans and the Zadokites. Dead Sea Scrolls are, in fact, obsessed with the violent conflict between the Hasmoneans and the Zadokites, so much so that the support of violence against Hasmoneans colors their writings in all genres: Community Rule Books, Bible Commentaries, Poetry, etc. In a sense, to be pro-Zadokite meant to support a violent overthrow of the Hasmoneans; there was no other way. Either the Hasmoneans occupied the top Jerusalem Temple leadership or the Zadokites; they could not share. And the Hasmoneans were not going to depart peacefully; in fact, it was the Hasmoneans who had slaughtered the Zadokites because they were afraid that they would try to claim their legitimacy.

Many influential Zadokites had to flee to Egypt and to desert areas to survive the sword of the Hasmoneans. Obviously, the Jew-on-Jew violence is justified in the purification of the Jerusalem Temple. What was at stake was the glory of God and if there were Jews supporting the Hasmonean power in Jerusalem, they had to be decimated as well by the Davidic messiah so that proper cultic worship can be carried out by legitimate representatives of God. And the Davidic messiah would be the righteous purger of Jerusalem and annihilator of fellow Jews because he would be properly instructed in the Word of God by legitimate priests. In other words, the Zadokites, the priests of King David's monarchy, will give instructions as to how to purge Jerusalem and bring back glory to the Jerusalem Temple that would be pleasing and acceptable to God. The Zadokites will teach the Davidic king God's ways. This is emphasized in Psalms of Solomon 17:35 as the Zadokite poet-composer of the Psalms of Solomon emphasis that a righteous king–one who is correctly taught about God – will reign in Jerusalem.

Psalms of Solomon 17:36 shows that this righteous Davidic king under instruction from righteous priests, the Zadokites, will lead the Jewish people on the road to holiness. Of course, the Davidic king himself cannot lead the people in holiness technically because he is a king and not a priest. It is the job of the priests to lead people into holiness although the king can protect righteous priests so that proper cultic worship is carried out and ritual purity preserved. Thus, verse 36 should be seen as empowering the Zadokite priests since it will be the Zadokite priests who carry out the cultic worship and sacrifices and lead the people in the instruction of God. In a sense, therefore, Psalms of Solomon 17:36 can be seen as instructing the future Davidic king to take his responsibility for people's holiness seriously. And of course, the fulfilment of this responsibility will entail safeguarding the positions of the legitimate priests of the Jerusalem Temple; namely, the Zadokites.

Psalms of Solomon 17:37 continues in the pro-Zadokite vein. How is it then that saying that the Davidic messiah-king will neither gather gold and silver for war nor prepare horses, riders, bow, and ships for war a pro-Zadokite statement? Obviously, on the surface it may not seem to be pro-Zadokite in any way. In fact, it may seem to hurt the Zadokite cause for the Davidic messiah not to have military powers. How will he bring about the military defeat of the Hasmoneans? Superficial reading ignores the historical reality. At the time of Zadokite poet-composer's writing, it was a fact that that Zadokites have lost power in Jerusalem; in fact, the Zadokites were fleeing for their lives and living in the desert. There must have been perception among Jews in Jerusalem that the Zadokites will never rise again and that their defeat was permanent. In fact, the Israeli army was now controlled by the Hasmoneans who also controlled the Jerusalem Temple. There was no way the Zadokites could access the Israeli army, and it was thought that without a strong army the Zadokites could not overtake the Jerusalem Temple.

In a way, Zadokites were leaders who have lost the following of their own people who traded their legitimacy for the glamorous new priestly family, the Hasmoneans. Not only did ordinary Jews in Jerusalem doubt the potential future rise of the Zadokites, there was doubt among the Zadokites to be sure. Especially among the young, it was hard to imagine that the ragtag group of people – no matter how legitimate they were–could conquer the strong and visible military force and defeat the Hasmoneans with ostentatious wealth that they lacked. Writing in this historical environment and in light of these prevailing perceptions, the Zadokite poet-composer felt the need to reassure both his enemies and his group that God will reinstate the Zadokites despite their apparent weakness and poverty. Thus, although they could not see a visible army commanded by a Davidic messiah, they should not doubt that there was a

Davidic messiah in training. And this Davidic messiah will not be preparing for war in the conventional way, so they should not be discouraged but have faith in the ultimate victory. Thus, even the belittling of the physical army can be seen as pro-Zadokite propaganda of sorts.

Psalms of Solomon 17:38 continues in this vein. Yes, the Davidic messiah does not have any military power or wealth but that's okay because God Himself is his protector. God will fight the wars of the Davidic messiah for him. Thus, this allowed the possibility that there was a Davidic messiah in training on the side of the Zadokites even though there was no visible army, power, or wealth on the side of the Zadokites. Besides encouraging the possibility of even a Davidic messiah-in-training on the side of the Zadokites in exile, the claim that the Davidic messiah will rely on the LORD Himself who is King had the effect of recalling the good old days of Israel. Of course, the Zadokite poet-composer is masterfully recalling the Old Testament passages criticizing the Israelites who asked for a king like the nations around them. God had promised that because the Israelites had asked for a king like the nations around them that the Israelites will suffer under the yolk of the king. A part of the Old Testament tradition, in fact, leads to the assumption that the downward course of Israelite history started with the Israelite request for a king like those kings of Gentile nations around them. Thus, the emphasis that the LORD Himself will be King is a key signifier to recall the collective memories of the Golden Era of ancient Israel and to trigger disloyalty to the Hasmonean dynasty that was like the monarchies of the Gentile nations around them.

The Hasmoneans did not like to emphasize the kingship of God since that detracted from their monarchical powers. They preferred that the Jews observed the laws of the state, rather than the laws of God, if the laws of God contradicted the laws of the state. There is a reason why the Hasmonean dynasty crucified hundreds of the Phariesees; the Hasmonean monarchs did not like the Pharisees who emphasized strict observation of the Mosaic Law, although they were not as strict in observance as the Zadokites and their supporters out in the Judean Desert. The Hasmoneans were, by in large, a secularlized, cultured (according to the ways of the world) rulers who disdained the Fundamentalism and religiousness of some Jews to emphasize keeping the laws of God as strictly as possible. Emphasizing that God is King made the people pay closer attention to the Bible and the laws of God contained therein, rather than ignore those laws in lieu of the Hasmonean nationalist program of "tolerance," Hellenization, and secularization of the public sphere to disenfranchise religious organizations vis-à-vis the state. The Zadokite poet-composer of the Psalms of Solomon knew the secularizing program of the Hasmoneans who were interested in separating church and the state in order to gain more power for themselves and he also knew that many of the Jews in the population had private, personal resentment against such aggressive Hellenization program although they may have not voiced their opinions in public, which favored political correctness and tolerance which were hallmarks of Hellenization.

The Zadokite poet-composer of the Psalms of Solomon used the key signifier of God as King to tap into popular discontent to propel a popular rebellion against the government, which he considered to be standing against the will of God for the people. It is not inconceivable that the rising friction between the religious elements of the population and the Hasmonean government was due in part to the efforts of the Zadokite poet-composer of the Psalms of Solomon. The Psalms of Solomon was a widely disseminated document in the Late Second Temple Period. Its composition in Greek allowed it to be widely distributed even among the Hellenized and educated as well as ultra religious Jews many of whom were competent in Greek given that Greek was basically the language of the educated in Palestine during the Late Second Temple Period. In other words, the key signifier of God as King and other key signifiers employed by the poet-composer of the Psalms of Solomon worked to galvanize the people against the Hasmonean government. The revolt against the Hasmoneans came not only among the religious elites of the country but among the masses. Hasmoneans found that their country continued to be fragmented and degenerated into civil war like states. Despite the radical Hellenization program, the Hasmoneans found that the people sided with the religious who wanted to privilege the Law of God. Thus, the Hasmonean dynasty tried to placate the people by incorporating ultra religious leaders who privileged the Law of God over secular government legislation. This is most evident in the privileging of the Pharisees in the government after the government crucified hundreds of them on the charge of treason against the state. The complete reversal of the government policy represented the recognition that the masses sympathized not with the government but with the ultra religious even though the masses tended not to be ultra religious themselves and even quite secular in their own personal life in practical matters.

Psalms of Solomon 17:39-46 continues the emphasis that the Davidic messiah is a righteous ruler who recognizes the ultimate Kingship of God over him and the people. Verse 42 emphasizes that the Davidic messiah depends on God. It is God who gives the Davidic messiah strength through the spirit of holiness. And it is God who gives the Davidic messiah understanding – the wisdom that only God Himself can give. Verse 43 further stresses that it is God who blesses the Davidic king and gives him might. And the Davidic messiah will not lose his hope in God, who is the source of his strength. Verse 44 asked the rhetorical question: Who can stand against this Davidic messiah? Of course the answer to the rhetorical question is that no one can stand against the Davidic messiah. For, the Davidic messiah is mighty in his works and finds strength in the fear of the LORD.

Psalms of Solomon 17:44 emphasizes that the source of strength and wisdom of the Davidic messiah is his faith in and fear of the LORD, and this emphasis is consistent with the Zadokite poet-composer of the Psalms of Solomon's efforts to legitimize the Zadokites through the legitimization of Davidic rulers. The current rulers of Jerusalem are thus contrasted with the ideal rulers of the Bible. For the fear of the LORD is the beginning of wisdom, and the Davidic messiah has this crucial element that sets him apart from the Hasmoneans who had no fear of God. Would those with fear of God usurp the office of the king, which rightfully belonged to the line of David? Would those with the fear of God usurp the office of the High Priest, which legitimately belonged to the Zadokites? Of course, such rulers who did not fear God could not rule justly or righteously. Palms of Solomon 17:41 highlights this point: the Davidic messiah is pure from sin – including those cultic violations and the Hasmonean disobedience to God's will that the line of David should be the eternal monarchy over Israel.Thus, it is this Davidic messiah who can rule over a mighty people. And it is this Davidic messiah who can chastise the princes who have gone wrong and punish them accordingly. It is this righteous Davidic messiah who submits to the Kingship of God who can overthrow sinners occupying the executive branch of the current government as well as the unrighteous leaders in the judiciary and legislative branches who refuse to submit to the Law of God. This righteous Davidic messiah has God's sanction to start a war on earth with the words of his mouth as the Psalms of Solomon 17:39 stresses. Of course, without a violent war, it would be impossible to purify the government in Jerusalem tainted with Hasmoneans and Hasmonean sympathizers.

Thus, the start of a revolutionary war was integral to a reformist vision of the Zadokite poet-composer of the Psalms of Solomon. In this apocalyptic outlook, the Zadokite poet-composer stands united with other Zadokites who were calling for the overthrow of the current government in the nation's capital to bring the nation back to God and proper worship of God. Of course, the Zadokite poet-composer of the Psalms of Solomon resented the separation of church and state that the Hasmoneans pushed against the plan of God as outlined in the Bible for believers. The Hasmoneans have to be overthrown because they were not interested in keeping proper cultic regulations and ritual purity; they were against upholding the Law of God in the matters of the state and in public spheres. This went against the revealed will of God as outlined in the Bible. Thus, Psalms of Solomon 17:45 emphasizes that the Davidic messiah – after his violent overthrow of the government in the capital–will rule over the people with faith in God and righteousness as defined by God's Law. In other words, the Zadokite poet-composer sees the obligation to uphold the Law of God and proper worship of God as fundamental responsibilities of the rulers of the land in the executive, judiciary, and legislative branches of the government. This is consistent with Old Testament theology and emphasis–as the majority of Jewish religious leaders and Christian theologians–both Catholic thinkers and Protestant Reformers–affirmed in their writings during most of the 2,000 years of Christian history in Europe. Even now, the State of Israel operates with recognition that God's Law should be the law of the land and many European nations essentially hold to this position. This highlights the highly populist nature of such a train of thought. And it was to the masses as well as intellectuals that the Zadokite poet-composers appealed to. Psalms of Solomon 17:46 also emphasizes the obligation of the ruler to rule under the authority of God, recognizing that his obligation as the nation's leader is to safeguard proper religious worship and the holiness of the nation according to the Law of God. The Zadokite poet-composer affirms that the Davidic messiah will obey the will of God as found in the Bible and rule in recognition of the Word of God in leading the people in the ways of holiness as prescribed by the Law of God. And the Zadokite poet-composer notes that ruling in this way will result in the lack of oppression.

Psalms of Solomon 17:47-51 further describes the apocalyptic Davidic messiah whom God will establish over Israel. Like verses 39-46, Psalms of Solomon 17:47-51 is pro-Zadokite propaganda. Verse 47 clearly emphasizes the divine appointment of the king over Israel. In other words, the Davidic messiah will be king over Israel because he is place over Israel by God Himself.

Psalms of Solomon 17:47-51 is aggressive pro-Zadokite propaganda. Verse 47 is pre-Zadokite by propping up the authority of the Davidic messiah. The Davidic messiah in the apocalyptic time should be king because he is appointed by God Himself. The very foundation of his majesty is based on divine appointment. It is important to note the difference between divine favor and divine appointment. Divine favor does not necessarily mean direct divine appointment. For instance, King Nebuchadnezzar was already a ruler when God favored him as the instrument of his judgment over Israelites and Jerusalem. Although from one vantage point, it can be argued that God had appointed King Nebuchadnezzar as king because God is the Creator and Sustainer of all things, the fact is that the biblical texts do not emphasize that God Himself made him king over the Babylonians. King Nebuchadnezzar was already a king over the Babylonians when God decided to use him as His instrument of judgment. Thus, it is safe to assume that God's direct appointment trumps any favoring of God who is already in power. In this light, verse 47 is important. Psalms of Solomon 17:47 emphasizes that it was God Himself who appointed the Davidic messiah as the king over Israel and the king's majesty is directly tied to God's personal appointment.

Of course, this is pro-Zadokite propaganda because there was no understanding that God Himself had appointed the Hasmonean king over Israel. In fact, there was wide perception in the Late Second Temple Period that the Hasmoneans have unjustly usurped the position of the king. After all, the Hasmoneans were priests. And the office of the High Priest and the office of the king were seen as distinct. The fact that the High Priest took the title of the king seemed contrary not only to the received tradition but also to the laws of God Himself. Thus, the poet-composer of the Psalms of Solomon was exploiting the wide-spread (even if muted) dissatisfaction among the Jewish populace regarding the usurpation of the royal position and title by the High Priest.

What compounded the problem was that the Hasmoneans were not even legitimate High Priests. The Hasmoneans had usurped the position of the High Priest from the Zadokites. Thus, in a sense, it was consistent with the nature of the Hasmoneans to usurp someone else's legitimate office. This is the propaganda behind the emphasis of Psalms of Solomon 17:47 that God Himself appointed the Davidic messiah as the king over Israel. Of course, when one emphasizes that the Davidic messiah is the rightful king over Israel, one is concurrently (in effect) emphasizing that the Zadokites are the rightful priests of Israel. Thus, arguing for the divine appointment of the Davidic king is like emphasizing the divine appointment of the Zadokite priest to the office of the High Priest.

And certainly there are ample Old Testament references to prop up the idea of the divine approval of the line of David. Not only is the eternal royal line of David emphasized in biblical texts thought to be originating from the First Temple Period, but this concept was also seen to be emphatic in Exilic literature and post-Exilic literature. King David and his line are the only legitimate kings over Israel and this was divine appointment, forever. Concurrently, the Zadokites were to be the High Priests of the Jerusalem Temple, forever. Of course, it is a foregone conclusion (in the minds of the Zadokites) that if a Davidic king was on the throne of Israel that a Zadokite priest would be the High Priest of the Jerusalem Temple.

Verse 48 continues in the emphasis that God Himself appoints and sustains the Davidic king. Psalms of Solomon 17:48 emphasizes that the Davidic king's words shall be purified above fine gold. Of course, it is assumed that it is God who purifies the words. The concept of God purifying the words is often associated with divine approval. For instance, David wrote in his poem that the refiner's fire (*ie.*, that of God) should purify him. The understanding is that God should purify him and his words so that he will speak justly, righteously, and in a way that is consistent with the will of God. God's fire purifying is a concept used by God's prophets as well. Isaiah the prophet describes himself as a person with unclean lips (and, therefore, unclean speech). Thus, God is seen as purifying his lips and his speech so that he may be worthy to carry out the will of God. The tradition of God refining purer than gold the lips or words of the king whom he appoints or the prophet whom he appoints is, in fact, ingrained in the Old Testament. Thus, this metaphor is consistent with the language of the Old Testament.

We see that the purification of the words is directly tied to the carrying out of God's will and plan. In the second part of Psalms of Solomon 17:48, the priest-composer of the Psalms of Solomon writes, the Davidic king will judge the congregation of Israel after his words are purified. And verse 48 emphasizes that the congregation will be comprised of the tribes of Israel that has been satisfied. As mentioned before, the emphasis on the tribes of Israel has to be seen as an emphasis on the Davidic line for royalty and the Zadokite line for the High Priest. Zadokites had a vested interest in emphasizing the pure bloodline because they were extremely cautious in maintaining a pure bloodline since their office of the High Priest depended on their bloodline. Of course, such an emphasis on pure bloodline was not very important for the Jews of the Late Second Temple Period since many of them intermarried during the Exile and it was nearly impossible to find a Jew with a pure bloodline by the time of the Late Second Temple Period. Hasmoneans, of course, had something to lose from the emphasis of tribes and pure bloodline because according to tradition and the Jewish Law, the king should be a descendant of David (in other words, of the bloodline of David). Obviously, the Hasmoneans were not descended from David so they were, in fact, illegitimate kings. So, the Hasmoneans had a vested interest to de-emphasize blood lineage and tribes of Israel. This explains, in part, their aggressive Hellenization. The Hasmoneans wanted the Jews to be diverted away from issues of bloodline, tribes, and Davidic lineage and focus on the universalism of humanity.

For many Jews, this suited them fine since they were of mixed blood and many could not frankly trace their lineage to a particular tribe. And since all the records were destroyed by the Babylonians when they sacked Jerusalem and killed most of its populace, there was no written document to account for blood lineage of almost all the Jews in the Exile. And during the Exile, even the element of Oral Tradition was hazy. Could you really believe that you were the tribe of Judah just because both of your parents said you were? Maybe they made it all up because it was glamorous to belong to the tribe of Judah. There were some Jewish parents who wanted to hide their dark past of predominant Gentile intermarriage among their forefathers especially since they themselves have re-discovered the Jewish religion and had committed to an orthodox Jewish way of life. There were many reasons why Jews perpetuated a lie – sometimes, they believed it; other times, they simply lied to cover up a shameful past. As far as the Jewish Law was concerned, without legitimate marriage certificate stamped by legitimate Jewish religious authorities, they could not affirm their identity. The problem, of course, was that many Jews married in civil marriages in the Exile. No one could verify their Jewish heritage. Furthermore, the authorities had been overthrown. Zadokites were on the run and the Hasmoneans had usurped power. How many Hasmoneans willingly abided by documents of the Hasmoneans is a point of contention. As far as we know, the Hasmoneans seemed to have secretly "shredded" (or burned) official documents of the Zadokites for fear that it can lend authenticity to the Zadokites on whose official authority the documents had been issued and policies made. The Hasmoneans were interested in propping up their authority. Not only were they afraid that they were not the legitimate rulers of Israel, they had real fear for factions that were still loyal to the Zadokites. Thus, the Hasmoneans destroyed religious documents – including many documents relating to blood lineage – of the Zadokites for their own political authority.

Thus, the Jews of the Late Second Temple Period could not affirm their Jewish lineage and heritage. For all they knew, their great grandparents were recent converts to Judaism and they had absolutely no Jewish heritage beyond them. In fact, historical records show that the majority of the Jews in Galilee were converts. There was aggressive proselytism in the Late Second Temple Period, and it was at this time that many Gentiles in Eretz Israel became Jews. This conversionist policy did not start with the Hasmoneans. It actually started with the Zadokites. But the Zadokites were not interested in keeping strict records of who converted because as far as they were concerned at the time, they were securely in power and such record-keeping was unnecessary. The Zadokites did not anticipate their overthrow by the Hasmoneans. It seemed like an impossibility given the secure power and the wealth of the Zadokites. And even the records kept were destroyed along with other Zadokite documents when Hasmoneans stormed into power in Jerusalem. They had to destroy any document that would lend Zadokites any legitimacy and power. They did not have the time to go through every document before destroying them. So, they destroyed Zadokite documents wholesale to safeguard their rule – including documents crucial to Jewish history and religion.

In fact, it was only after the Hasmoneans took power, that the Zadokites began to emphasize their bloodlineage as it was tied to their legitimacy. In the same way, they began to emphasize the tribes of Israel because it relates to bloodlineage and emphasis on legitimacy based on blood lineage.

Even though the Jews of the Late Second Temple Period really did not know their tribe or if they even belonged to a tribe or if they were descended from converts, they glamorized the idea of being descended from Abraham. Thus, there is increased writing about Abraham and the Patriarchs in the Late Second Temple Period. Now that the Jewish commonwealth was secure, ironically Jews wanted to discover their roots. But frankly, Jews of the Late Second Temple Period had absolutely no way to ascertain blood lineage from almost everyone except for the Zadokites and those of the line of David. Even in these regards, there was an element of uncertainty. There was no documentary trail, and oral tradition was far too unreliable as to be useful in any way.

This can be likened to Jews of America. Jews of America often like to describe Jewish identity in terms of bloodlineage (through the mother). But this is based on non-historical factors. There is no record of the Jews extending 2,000 years of history in the diaspora. There is absolutely no record of the tribes of Israel. In fact, most Jews cannot trace their bloodlineage beyond three generations. It is possible that all their family members are all descended from converts to Judaism in 1800s when many converted to Judaism. And throughout 2,000 years of Diaspora history, there have been many waves of conversions to Judaism in different parts of Europe and Arab lands. There is no historical proof from a blood lineage of the Jews. This is conclusively proven from one historical document that survives that recalls the vote on this issue. The Great Sanhedrin of Nepoleon confirmed that Jewish identity was a religious identity and not racial identity. Of course, this was the only conclusion the great rabbis of Europe could make at the time because they did not have documents to account for the lineage of nearly all of the Jews in the synagogues.

But modern Jews of America would like to believe that somehow they are linked by blood to the twelve tribes of Israel and even to Abraham. Such a desire for link to the past existed in the Late Second Temple Period. Many people then in Israel as many Jews in America now liked to believe this point and emphasize this point even though there was no real historical support for the emphasis on blood lineage. But Zadokites found such reason for blood lineage useful to exploit. Jews wanted to be linked to the past? Then, the Zadokites were going to feed them what they wanted. They were going to promise renewal and rededication of the tribes of Israel. Of course, all of this was in return for putting Zadokites back into power.

Psalms of Solomon 17:49 continues the pro-Zadokite propaganda in this vein. The poet-composer of the Psalms of Solomon props up the authority of the Zadokite priesthood by propping up the authority of the Davidic king. When the poet-composer of the Psalms of Solomon describes in verse 49 that the Davidic king's words will be like the words of the "holy ones," he is basically saying that the Davidic king's words will be the words of priest, who are seen as "the holy ones." Thus, basically, the Zadokite poet-composer is stating that the Davidic king will speak in agreement with the Zadokite priest and that he will prop up their authority. In other words, as the congregation of Israel is gathered, the Zadokite priests lead them in cultic worship and proper ritual observation. In this context, the Davidic king will speak in a manner consistent with proper cultic worship and ritual observance.

This, of course, can be seen as an attack on the Hasmoneans who we thought to have usurped the Jerusalem Temple. Not only did they usurp the office which was not rightfully theirs, they were leading Israelites in a path that did not have approval of God. How was this evident? The Zadokite poet-composer's argument was that this is self-evident in the fact that the tribes of Israel were not gathered in a congregation sanctified according to the rules of the Torah. The Torah clearly called for a tribal division of Eretz Israel and cultic worship that was tied to tribal association. Any Jew going to the Jerusalem Temple and living a life as a Jew in the Late Second Temple Period could see that what was mandated by the Torah was not happening.

Psalms of Solomon 17:50 clearly emphasizes this point. The Zadokite poet-composer stresses that the time that the tribes will be gathered as tribes is not the present. Rather, such a time will be in the future. Thus, the Zadokite poet-composer calls for blessings of the Jews who will be born at the time in the future when God will appoint the Davidic king over Israel and the tribes will be gathered as tribes in a holy congregation. This future, of course, is the eschatological and apocalyptic future.

It is further important to note that the Zadokite poet-composer stresses the point that the gathered tribes are those that are gathered by God Himself (Psalms of Solomon 17:50). Thus, not only will God Himself appoint a Davidic messiah as a king over Israel, but God Himself will also gather the tribes of Israel. This is a very important point since, as explained earlier, the tribes of Israel were completely lost. No one really knew which tribes to which they belonged to or whether if they belonged to any tribes at all. There were many converts to Judaism and profusion of intermarriages. To an ordinary Jew, it seemed impossible that the tribes of Israel could be identified and people could be gathered in a congregation according to the tribes of Israel.

But what is impossible with humans is possible with God. That is why the emphasis by the Zadokite poet-composer is significant. He is in effect stating: "Yes, of course, you can't imagine the Jews being gathered according to their tribes because it seems humanly impossible. But this will happen at the apocalyptic age because God Himself will do it." Of course, such a statement was meant to solicit the support of the Jews of the Late Second Temple Period. They were to side with the Zadokites instead of the Hasmoneans if they desired to be a part of the glorious apocalyptic age when God Himself would drive out the errant Jews and the Hasmoneans from the Jerusalem Temple and the city of Jerusalem and establish rightful heir to the throne of David in Jerusalem and the priests of David, the Zadokites.

This apocalyptic picture is completely consistent with the pro-Zadokite propaganda found in the Dead Sea Scrolls. In the Qumran scrolls, the Zadokites and their supporters in the Judean Desert called for an eschatological war between the Children of Light and the Children of Darkness. The Children of Light are the supporters of the Zadokite Teacher of Righteousness. The Children of Darkness are the Hasmonean Wicked Priest and their supporters who kicked out the Zadokites from Jerusalem. In the eschatological war, God's Davidic messiah will wage war against the Jews currently occupying Jerusalem and their Gentile allies. After killing these errant Jews and their Gentile allies in a spectacular apocalyptic war, God will instate the Davidic messiah as a king over Israel and there will be a *tikkun olam* according to the principles of Torah. Since God would be the author of this violent apocalyptic war, the victory is guaranteed. And since God is the arranger of the new order after the apocalyptic war, the Israelites will be arranged according to their tribes.

Such an apocalyptic vision was attractive to many ordinary Jews on the street. Even if they themselves were not particularly religious, they hoped for something they could believe in. A Davidic messiah who would restore all things after the Great Purge seemed to be a type of utopia among ordinary Jews wary of scandal, among the political leadership and the religious leaders. It is no accident that John Collins refers to the Late Second Temple Period as rife with "apocalyptic imagination." It was indeed a period of profusion of apocalyptic writing. Apocalyptic writings were not merely in the fringes of the Israeli society, like in the Negev Desert; rather, the apocalyptic imagination took hold of the general population and made an indelible mark on the literature and thinking of the Late Second Temple Period as a whole. Thus, it is not surprising that aggressive apocalyptic thought marks the quintessential Late Second Temple Period document of the Psalms of Solomon.

In this light, it is easy to understand the call of Psalms of Solomon 17:51. When the Zadokite poet-composer of the Psalms of Solomon calls for deliverance from the "abomination of unhallowed adversaries," he is not referring to the Gentiles, primarily. Rather, the primary target of the Zadokite poet-composer's apocalyptic imagination is fellow Jews. The Jews–Hasmoneans and their supporters–who usurped the offices of the royalty and the High Priesthood had to be killed. And it was God who was going to send the Davidic messiah to kill the errant Jews in order to purify the Jerusalem Temple and establish a holy congregation according to their tribes to carry out proper cultic worship and ritual observance. In other words, the Zadokite poet-composer was calling for a violent civil war among the Jews as the Qumran Zadokites did in their writings. It was impossible to purify the Jerusalem Temple and the Holy City according to Torah and Mitzvah unless the current Jerusalem leaders and their supporters were first annihilated.

The conclusion of the chapter and the verse (Psalms of Solomon 17:51) emphasizes this point. The LORD is king from everlasting to everlasting. The Hasmoneans who are calling themselves king are not really the king; God is the king. This is a way to give permission to all Jews to abrogate their allegiance to the king, the state, and the army. Jews of the Hasmonean period would be right to take up arms against the so-called God's anointed because they were really not God's anointed. On the authority of God's kingship, even, Jews could take up arms and start violent civil war against the current government. All Jews were released, in effect, from their oath of allegiance to Israel and the king of Israel. Their allegiance was to God and God alone. This secret service who surrounded the commander-in-chief was called upon to execute him in allegiance to God the King. Even citizens of Israel were called upon to overthrow their government in allegiance to God the King. Israeli soldiers and army battalions were to wage war against their own government in allegiance to God the King.

Psalms of Solomon 17 must be seen as an aggressive pro-Zadokite propaganda calling for reform through violent means. In effect, it was calling on "true Jews" to annihilate errant Jews who were desecrating the House of God and country which belonged to God. The Zadokite poet-composer saw no other way to reform the country except through violent annihilation of fellow Jews. This is consistent with the apocalyptic imagination that marked the Late Second Temple Period.

Bibliography

Argall, Randal A., Beverly A. Bow, and Rodney A. Werline (Editors). *For a Later Generation: The Transformation of Tradition in Israel, Early Judaism, and Early Christianity*. Harrisburg: Trinity International Press, 2000.

Atkinson, Kenneth. *An Intertextual Study of the Psalms of Solomon: Pseudepigrapha*. Lewiston: The Edwin Mellen Press, 2000.

Chancey, Mark A. *The Myth of a Gentile Galilee*. Cambridge: Cambridge University Press, 2002.

Collins, John J. *Apocalypticism in the Dead Sea Scrolls*. London: Routledge, 1997.

Collins, John J., and Robert A. Kugler (Editors). *Religion in the Dead Sea Scrolls*. Grand Rapids: William B. Eerdmans Publishing Company, 2000.

Davila, James R.. *The Dead Sea Scrolls as Background to Postbiblical Judaism and Early Christianity: Papers from an International Conference at St. Andrews in 2001*. Leiden: Brill, 2003.

De Jonge, Marinus. *Jewish Eschatology, Early Christian Christology and the Testament of the Twelve Patriarchs*. Leiden: E. J. Brill, 1991.

De Jonge, Marinue (Editor). *Outside the Old Testament*. Cambridge: Cambridge University Press, 1985.

Falk, Daniel K., Florentino García Martínez, and Eileen Schuller (Editors). *Sapiential, Liturgical and Poetic Texts from Qumran: Proceedings of the Third Meeting of the International Organization for Qumran Studies, Oslo 1998*. Leiden: Brill, 2000.

Goodblatt, David, Avital Pinnick, and Daniel R. Schwartz (Editors). *Historical Perspectives: From the Hasmoneans to Bar Kokhba in Light of the Dead Sea Scrolls: Proceedings of the Fourth International Symposium of the Orion Center for the Study of the Dead Sea Scrolls and Associated Literature, 27-31 January, 1999*. Leiden: Brill, 2001.

Hann, Robert R. *The Manuscript History of the Psalms of Solomon.* Chico: Scholars Press, 1982.

Kim, Heerak Christian. *Hebrew, Jewish, and Early Christian Studies: Academic Essays.* Cheltenham: The Hermit Kingdom Press, 2005.

Kim, Heerak Christian. *Key Signifier as Literary Device: Its Definition and Function in Literature and Media.* Lewiston: The Edwin Mellen Press, 2006.

Kim, Heerak Christian. *The Jerusalem Tradition in the Late Second Temple Period: Diachronic and Synchronic Developments Surrounding Psalms of Solomon 11.* Lanham: University Press of America, Inc., 2007.

Knight, George A. F. *Tradition and Theology in the Old Testament.* London: SPCK, 1977.

Kraus, Hans-Joachim. *Worship in Israel: A Cultic History of the Old Testament.* Translated by Geoffrey Buswell. Richmond: John Knox Press, 1965.

Kugel, James L. *The Idea of Biblical Poetry: Parallelism and Its History.* New Haven: Yale University Press, 1981.

Kwon, Hyuk Seung, *The Zion Tradition and the Kingdom of God: A Study on the Zion Traditions as Relevant to the Understanding of the Concept of the Kingdom of God in the New Testament* (Ph.D. thesis, Hebrew University of Jerusalem, 1998).

Lichtenberger, Hermann. *Studien zum Menschenbild in Texten der Qumrangemeinde.* Göttingen: Vandenboeck & Ruprecht, 1980.

Marinez, Florentino Garcia. *Qumran and Apocalyptic: Studies on the Aramaic Texts from Qumran.* Leiden: E. J. Brill, 1992.

McConville, J. G., and J. G. Millar (Editors). *Time and Place in Deuteronomy.* Sheffield: Sheffield Academic Press, 1994.

Mowinckel, Sigmund. *The Psalms in Israel's Worship.* Translated by D. R. Ap-Thomas. Grand Rapids: William B. Eerdmans Publishing Company, 2004.

Nickelsburg, George W. E. *Jewish Literature between the Bible and the Mishnah: A Historical and Literary Introduction.* Philadelphia: Fortress Press, 1981.

Rowley, H. H. *Worship in Ancient Israel: Its Forms and Meaning.* Philadelphia: Fortress Press, 1967.

Ryle, Herbert Edward, and Montague Rhodes James. *Psalms of the Pharisees Commonly Called The Psalms of Solomon.* Eugene: Wipf & Stock Publishers, 2006.

Sacchi, Paolo. *The History of the Second Temple Period.* Sheffield: Sheffield Academic Press, 2000.

Sanders, E. P. *Paul, the Law, and the Jewish People.* Minneapolis: Fortress Press, 1983.

Sanders, E. P. *Paul and Palestinian Judaism: A Comparison of Patterns of Religion.* Minneapolis: Fortress Press, 1977.

Schäfer, Peter. *The History of the Jews in the Greco-Roman World.* London: Routledge, 2003.

Schiffman, Lawrence H. (Editor). *Archaeology and History in the Dead Sea Scrolls: The New York University Conference in Memory of Yigael Yadin.* Sheffield: Sheffield Academic Press, 1990.

Schüpphaus, Joachim. *Die Psalmen Salomos: Ein Zeugnis Jerusalemer Theologie und Frömmigkeit in der Mitte des vorchristlichen Jahrhunderts.* Leiden: E. J. Brill, 1977.

Schürer, Emil. *The History of the Jewish People in the Age of Jesus Christ (Volume 2).* Revised and Edited by Geza Vermes, Fergus Millar, and Matthew Black. Edinburgh: T. & T. Clark, 1979.

Talmon, Shemaryahu. *King, Cult and Calendar in Ancient Israel: Collected Studies.* Leiden: E. J. Brill, 1986.

Thiede, Carsten Peter. *The Dead Sea Scrolls and the Jewish Origin of Christianity.* New York: Palgrave, 2000.

Trafton, Joseph L. *The Syriac Version of the Psalms of Solomon: A Critical Evaluation.* Atlanta: Scholars Press, 1985.

Ulrich, Eugene, and James Vanderkam (Editors). *The Community of the Renewed Covenant.* Notre Dame: University of Notre Dame Press, 1994.

Van Seters, John. *Abraham in History and Tradition.* New Haven: Yale University Press, 1975.

Weise, Manfred. *Kultzeiten und kultischer Bundesschluss in der "Ordensregel" vom Toten Meer.* Leiden: E. J. Brill, 1961.

Xeravits, Géza G. *King, Priest, Prophet: Positive Eschatological Protagonists of the Qumran Library.* Leiden: Brill, 2003.

Yadin, Yigael. *The Message of the Scrolls.* London: Weidenfeld and Nicolson, 1957.

Zimmermann, Johannes. *Messianische Texte aus Qumran: Königliche, priesterliche un prophetische Messiasvorstellungen in den Schriftfunden von Qumran.* Tübingen: Mohr Siebeck, 1998.

"Prohibition Imperative in Septuagint Greek"

The Septuagint's use of καυχάσθω, which in form is a third person singular imperative in the aorist, in Jeremiah 9:23 is irregular. This led me to an investigation of the use of imperatives in Greek, and I am happy to share my research with you. William Watson Goodwin's *Syntax of the Moods and Tenses of the Greek Verb* provides a good definition of the imperative: "The imperative expresses a command, exhortation, entreaty, or prohibition."[1] In terms of usage, the imperative is the least used mood in Greek.[2]

And the imperative is expressed via the usage of subjunctive and imperative forms in Greek. The first person imperative is expressed only in the subjunctive form, both in positive imperatives and negative imperatives.[3] Both present subjunctive and aorist forms are used. Goodwin states that they express the same tense and their only difference is that "the present expresses an action in its *duration*, that is, as *going on* or *repeated* while the aorist expresses simply its *occurrence*."[4]

In the second and the third person, positive imperatives are expressed via the use of imperative form in the Greek, both in present and aorist. However, in negative imperatives, or prohibitions, there is a difference. Prohibitions can be expressed in the negative via the use of μή with the present imperative form in Greek or the aorist subjunctive form.[5] The use of the Greek aorist imperative form is very rare to the extent that it can be seen as irregular. In *The Iliad*, there are only 3 aorist imperative forms attested for prohibitions out of 125 prohibitions (or negative imperatives). That is only 2.4 per cent of the

---

[1] William Watson Goodwin, *Syntax of the Moods and Tenses of the Greek Verb* (New York: St. Martin's Press, 1889, 1965), p. 6.
[2] Yves Duhoux, *Le verbe grec ancient: Éléments de morphologie et de syntaxe historique* (Louven: Peeters, 1992), p. 237.
[3] Duhoux, p. 206.
[4] Goodwin, p. 22.
[5] Goodwin, p. 89.

prohibitions in *The Iliad*. In *The Odyssey*, there are only 2 aorist imperative forms attested for prohibition out of 84 prohibitions. That is only 2.38 per cent of the prohibitions in *The Odessey*. In total, there are 5 attestations of the Greek aorist imperative form in prohibitions found in Homer out of 209 prohibitions. That's 2.39 per cent. This reality in Homer is in fact indicative of Greek grammar as further shown in Sophocles and Attic orators. In Sophocles, there are only 4 attestations of the Greek aorist imperative form out of 117 prohibitions. That is only 3.41 per cent. In the writings of Attic orators, there are only 6 attestations of the Greek aorist imperative form out of 384 prohibitions. That is only 1.56 per cent of all prohibitions in the writings of Attic orators.[6] The rarity of the aorist imperative form usage in Greek prohibitions marks it as an irregular usage. I would argue that its rare usage attests to its development via analogy to the present imperative form usage and may even indicate a grammatical error.

Because there is really no sense of tense but only of aspect which distinguishes the present from the aorist, the existence of the Greek imperative form (in the present) and the Greek subjunctive form (in the aorist) for expressing prohibition points to difference in intensity. In Greek prohibitions, the present imperative form expresses a stronger prohibition than the aorist subjunctive form. Jean Humbert writes: "A la différence de l'impératif, qui interdit une *action déjà commence*, ou pose *en principe* une interdiction, le subjonctif de défense, *qui n'est pas employé en dehors de aoriste*, exprime une sorte d'avertissement negative..."[7] Thus, for Greek prohibitions, the subjunctive form (in the aorist) allows for choice, whereas the Greek imperative form (in the present) does not.

This leads us to the question regarding καυχάσθω in Jeremiah 9:23. Why is it that we find the imperative form in the aorist and not in the present as it is normative in Greek prohibitions? I would argue that it was simply a mistake of the LXX translator. He wanted to use the Greek imperative form rather than the subjunctive form because he wanted to set down a principle, a strong command, which the subjunctive form could not achieve as it is a weaker prohibition form that leaves room for choice. However, the LXX translator was disturbed by the fact that duration expressing present "tense" lacked the finality of the once-for-all aspect of the aorist "tense." He wanted the prohibitive command to be an order with an impending-doom scenario finality to it and the use of the aorist aspect coupled with the imperative form allowed him to achieve the semantic force. In a sense, therefore, LXX translator sacrificed syntactic norms in lieu of his semantic intent.

---

[6] Duhoux, p. 207.
[7] Jean Humbert, *Syntaxe Greque* (Paris: Libraire C. Klincksieck, 1954), p. 114.

Bibliography

Duhoux, Yves. *Le verbe grec ancient: Éléments de morphologie et de syntaxe historiques.* Leuven: Peeters, 1992.

Goodwin, William Watson. *Syntax of the Mood and Tenses of the Greek Verb.* New York: St. Martin's Press, 1889, 1965.

Humbert, Jean. *Syntax Greque.* Paris: Librairie C. Klincksieck, 1954.

Smyth, Herbert Weir. *Greek Grammar.* Cambridge: Harvard University Press, 1920, 1984.

"Beloved as the Source of Redemption: Toni Morrison's Contribution to the Phenomenon of Scripturalization"[1]

I am convinced that more conjunctive studies must be done on the concept of scripturalization as a phenomenon. This will help us better understand "scripture" and its relationship to the community which values it. There are shared traits in the scripturalization process of diverse communities throughout history as comparative religions scholars and anthropologists have shown. It is my argument that understanding the concept of scripturalization in the African-American community will help better understand scripturalization in ancient societies, including that of the earliest Christians. In this paper, I will explain the process of scripturalization in Toni Morrison's "Beloved" with the understanding that there is active scripturalization in form and content of the literary work. I will particularly focus on the character of Beloved and her redemptive role. I would assert that Professor Morrison utilizes the genre elements of "the fantastic" effectively to present Beloved as a source of redemption. Tzvetan Todorov's *The Fantastic: A Structural Approach to a Literary Genre* and Rosemary Jackson's *Fantasy, the Literature of Subversion* will serve in the identification of genre elements of the fantastic. I will argue that Beloved's redemptive role is significant in light of African-American history of slavery and oppression. Understanding the way Beloved functions in the scripturalization process will shed light on the phenomenon of scripturalization. Based on this paper, presented at the Society of Biblical Literature Annual Meeting in 2006, I intend to show at a future Society of Biblical Literature conference how this opens the door to better understanding of scripturalization in the New Testament.

---

[1] This academic paper was presented at the African-American Biblical Hermeneutics Section of the 2006 Annual Meeting of Society of Biblical Literature in Washington, DC, 2006.

In The Fantastic: A Structural Approach to a Literary Genre, Tzvetan Todorov defines fantasy, or "the fantastic," as a hesitation. It is the moment of uncertainly between the marvellous and the uncanny. This uncertainty exists on two levels; namely, on the part of the characters within the narrative of the story itself and on the part of the reader who reads the story.[1] Thus, if the character in the story is described as uncertain whether something is marvellous or uncanny, he is experiencing "the fantastic." Often, the reader shares in the experience of the characters in the narrative in "the fantastic." However, it is possible that the narrative may resolve "the fantastic" for the reader of the story, but the characters within the narrative may be suspended in the realm of "the fantastic." Thus, the experience of "the fantastic" is not equally shared by the characters in the narrative and the reader. In fact, it is possible for "the fantastic" to be never resolved for the characters in the narrative, although it is for the reader. And it is possible that the characters in the story may be described as having resolved his hesitation and decide that something is uncanny or marvellous within the narrative itself, but the reader is still left in the state of hesitation of deciding for himself. Thus, for Todorov, fantasy or "the fantastic" is not a stagnant category and can even be described as "genre elements" rather than a genre. In other words, the episode in the novel that describes the hesitation of the characters can be described with the term "the fantastic" but the moment that the hesitation is resolved within the narrative, the genre element of "the fantastic" ends.[2] Thus, even if the novel or a literary work is not a fantasy as a whole, it can contain genre elements of "the fantastic" or fantasy. Todorov's contribution to the study of fantasy, therefore, is in the possibility he opens up for studying genre elements of the fantastic in any written literature or spoken art form, such as films.

Whereas Todorov's contribution to the genre of fantasy can be seen as structural, Rosemary Jackson's contribution to the study of the genre of fantasy is in the area of function. Rosemary Jackson's *Fantasy, the Literature of Subversion* argues that fantasy as a genre is necessarily subversive. Jackson argues that fantasy pushes the boundaries of what is considered "real" in the society as well as what is deemed to be normal or normative.[3] Thus, Jackson describes the genre of fantasy as pushing the boundaries of a society. Often, therefore, the genre of fantasy is employed as a means to protest the norms of society or societal boundaries.[4] This is the case whether there is intentionality to fantasy writing or not; functionally, the genre of fantasy pushes the limits of society—in the way things are perceived to be real or normal.

---

[1] Todorov, *The Fantastic*, p. 41.
[2] Todorov, *The Fantastic*, p. 157.
[3] Rosemary Jackson, *Fantasy, the Literature of Subversion* (London: Methuen, 1981), p. 51.
[4] Jackson, *Fantasy*, p. 3.

Taking Todorov and Jackson together, we have a holistic definition of fantasy, or "the fantastic," which can be used to understand the process of scripturalization of texts, either written or spoken. In this academic paper delivered at the "African-American Biblical Hermeneutics Section" of the Society of Biblical Literature Annual Meeting 2006 in Washington DC during Thanksgiving time, I will focus on the process of scripturalization via the use of the genre of fantasy in African-American literature – in particular, in the novel *Beloved* by Toni Morrison.

There is no doubt that Toni Morrison's novel *Beloved* functions as a type of African-American scripture. When the Pulitzer Prize committee passed over the novel for the prize, the whole African-American literary community rose up in the way that Muslims rose up in protest against the Mohammed cartoons. The African-American community took non-recognition of *Beloved* as an insult to their personal identity and the honor of the African-American community.[5] Even then, Toni Morrison's *Beloved* had a status of a scripture. Since then, Oprah Winfrey brought the African-American scripture to the general audience by making a movie ("Beloved," 1998) about it. Oprah Winfrey called reading *Beloved* "a spiritual odyssey."[6] And even now, Toni Morrison's *Beloved* has the status of a scriptural text in the study of African-American literature, culture, and history. Toni Morrison's *Beloved* has been honored with the Nobel Prize for Literature. And Toni Morrison has been given an esteemed academic post at Princeton University to carry on her message and African-American scriptural exegesis of the history, experience, and literature of African-Americans. Toni Morrison's *Beloved* is now recognized by African-Americans as well as those outside of the community as an African-American scripture *par excellence* of the history and experience of African-Americans.

It is, therefore, appropriate for me to choose Toni Morrison's *Beloved* to examine the process of scripturalization in African-American literature. *Beloved* is quintessentially African-American in scripturalizaton[7] which opens the door to understanding scripturalization in all African-American literature.[8] In a sense,

---

[5] This discontent is well expressed by Nicole Wilkinson: "Writing is one of the weapons belonging to whites, and to read is to invite voices into the reader's head" (Nicole Wilkinson, "'The Getting of Names': Anti-Intertextuality and the Unread Bible in Toni Morrison's *Song of Solomon* and *Beloved*," *Semeia* 69/70 <1995, pp. 235-246>, p. 236).

[6] "Oprah Winfrey and Beloved," BBC News interview (Friday, March 5, 1999).

[7] Dwight N. Hopkins writes: "The experience of enslaved African Americans, in line with our understanding of religious culture, indicate that the question of ultimate concern are embodied, embedded, or incarnated, if you will, in the everyday life represented by manifold sources" (Dwight N. Hopkins, "Theological Mind and Cultural Studies: Slave Religious Culture as a Heuristic," *Changing Conversations: Religious Reflection & Cultural Analysis*, eds. Dwight N. Hopkins and Sheila Davaney <New York: Routledge, 1996, pp. 162-180>, p. 167).

[8] Carol Iannone describes Toni Morrison's novels as "in classic plight-and-protest style" that is seen to characterize African-American literature and African-American identity

we can refer to Toni Morrison's *Beloved* as the "Gospels" of the African-American community.

When we examine Toni Morrison's *Beloved*, we see that the genre element of "the fantastic," or fantasy, is proactively utilized. Although most of us are aware of the story, it would be helpful to briefly describe the story to provide the contextual framework. The main character of the story is Beloved, a ghost who takes a human form. Beloved is the ghost of the daughter whom Sethe killed during the days of slavery because she did not want her daughter falling into the hands of white slave owners. The story takes place eighteen years after the murder at a time when slavery is abolished and Sethe is living in Ohio with her daughter. Sethe is shunned by the African-American community in her area because of the fact that she killed her own daughter. Beloved, the personified ghost of Sethe's dead daughter, enters Sethe's life and comes to live in her home. Later, Beloved tries to kill Sethe. The African-American community comes to understand why Sethe killed her daughter during slavery times and comes together as a community to protect Sethe against the ghost of her daughter. The story ends in a happy note with the reconciliation of Sethe to the African-American community and to Paul D, her lover, who had left her when he found out about her killing her own daughter. Like the African-American community, Paul D comes to see the justification of Sethe's actions in light of the evils of slavery.

Obviously, the genre element of the fantastic in the story is Beloved, the ghost of Sethe's murdered daughter. The character itself is shrouded in mystery. Is Beloved really the dead daughter of Sethe? Nicole Wilkinson describes Beloved as "mistaken for a natural person for much of the book...."[9] Maybe she is just familiar with the story of the murdered baby and pretending to be her personification.[10] Although within the narrative, Beloved's identity as the embodiment of the dead daughter is clear, the reader is left with a hesitation as to the identity of Beloved. It is this hesitation of the identity of Beloved that fulfils the criterion for the genre of the fantastic which Todorov has outlined. And the hesitation regarding Beloved exists throughout the story and helps to focus the reader's attention on the identity of Beloved.

This is important because Beloved stands at the center of the scritpuralization process. Beloved is a character in the story, but Beloved is much more than that. Beloved represents countless African-American daughters and sons who were deserted by their mother on account of slavery. In the case of

---

(Carol Iannone, "Toni Morrison's Career," *Commentary* Vol. 84 No. 6 <December 1987, pp. 59-63>, pp. 59-60).
[9] Wilkinson, "The Getting of Names," p. 242.
[10] Elizabeth B. House, "Toni Morrison's Ghost: The Beloved Who Is Not Beloved," *Critical Essays on Toni Morrison's Beloved*, ed. Barbara H. Solomon (New York: G. K. Hall & Co., 1998, pp. 117-126), p. 117.

Sethe, she herself murdered her own daughter to protect her from slavery.[11] Although this may represent the most extreme form of desertion of a daughter, there were many other types of desertions done in the context of slavery. There were many African-American women who abandoned their children born as the result of rape by white slave owners. Even Sethe's mother abandoned all her children who were born of a white father. She only kept the child born of a black father.[12] Half-white children were also African-Americans because they would never be accepted in the white society as white. These African-Americans were the product of the oppression of slavery which allowed white men to treat African-American women like chattel and property and do whatever they liked to them, including invading their bodies and raping them at will. Just as the blame for the murder of Sethe's daughter is placed on the evils of slavery, the abandonment of half-white African-American children by their parents are somewhat justified by the evils of slavery. Beloved, therefore, represents all the African-American children who were abandoned by their parents during slavery times due to evils of slavery.

The fact that Beloved remains in the realm of the fantastic allows her to take a symbolic, representative role more fully. A real, tangible identity has a way of limiting the potential, or expandability, of a person or an individual. But the fantastic element suspending Beloved in a space of hesitation between the uncanny and the marvellous allows her to represent limitless possibilities. Thus, besides representing countless children abandoned or killed by their own parents due to the evils of slavery, Beloved also represents many Africans who were killed on the way to slavery.[13] Toni Morrison numbers them as more than 60 million. There were Africans captured in Africa for slavery. Many Africans were killed in the process of capture. Of those Africans who were captured for slavery, many died in captivity because of inhumane conditions in which they were kept. Out of those who made it alive to the time of boarding of slave ships, many died at sea as African slaves were crowded together in these slave ships and treated worse than animals. And many more Africans died after landing in the United States of America en route to their slavery destinations. All these Africans marked for slavery but did not make it to their slavery destination are represented by Beloved.

Beloved as the fantasy character, therefore, contributes integrally to the scripturalizing *Tendenz* in Toni Morrison's literary narrative. But Beloved does not only represent structural embodiment of the fantastic in Toni Morrison's novel. Beloved also serves the functional aspect of the genre of fantasy

---

[11] Toni Morrison, *Beloved: A Novel* (New York: Vintage Books, 2004), p. 236.
[12] Gurleen Grewal, *Circles of Sorrow, Lines of Struggle* (Baton Rouge: Louisiana State University Press, 1998), p. 101.
[13] Terry Otten, *The Crime of Innocence in the Fiction of Toni Morrison* (Columbia: University of Missouri Press, 1989), p. 83.

described by Jackson. Beloved provides the opportunity to push the limits of reality and, more importantly, of the norms of society.

Of course, the reality of the society that Beloved pushes on the surface level (*peshat*) is to present the possibility of a ghost being personified in Beloved. In a sense, therefore, the message proffered by Beloved is that just as there may be a possibility for a ghost to come back to punish the mother for killing her, there is the possibility of the ghosts of African-American slaves to come back and punish the slave owners and the present-day equivalent of oppressors of the African-American community. Thus, Beloved functions as a fantastic hope for making the evils of slavery right and for justice to be done not only for the past wrongs but present wrongs against the African-American community. It can be seen as a vengeance-is-mine-saith-the-Lord type of hope embodied in the fantastic person of Beloved in the narrative.

Besides the obvious and surface function of Beloved serving the fantastic role of pushing the realms of reality as a ghost, Beloved represents a fantastic opportunity to subvert the perception of normalcy based on dominant cultural values. Thus, Beloved functions as a fantastic element of subversion of societal norms. The dominant culture has certain regulations that dictate what the societal value is. Thus, killing a daughter is wrong. And this dominant value is initially accepted by the African-American community in Sethe's Ohio in the literary narrative, at first. However, as Beloved enters the narrative and comes into confrontation with Sethe, the dominant ethical position is questioned.[14] The African-American community comes to understand that more evil than the murder of one's own daughter is the evil of slavery itself.[15] Thus, Beloved, who represents the daughter whom Sethe killed to prevent her from falling into the hands of white slave owners, become the source of Sethe's acceptance back into African-American community.[16] In other words, if Beloved did not enter Sethe's life, then she would have continued to be ostracized by the African-American community, which subscribed to the dominant ethical position that killing of one's child is evil. Beloved as the fantastic genre element provides the opportunity for the characters of the literary narrative to understand evil in

---

[14] Wendy Harding and Jacky Martin, *A World of Difference: An Inter-Cultural Study of Toni Morrison's Novels* (Westport: Greenwood Press, 1994), p. 113.

[15] Otten, *The Crime of Innocence*, p. 82.

[16] To a large extent, it is possible to understand *Beloved* as representing Toni Morrison's feminist theology. Susan Corey Everson's comments about *Tar Baby* is relevant for *Beloved* as well: "With this novel, Morrison has contributed to shaping what Carol Christ has called a new sacred story for women, a story which charts the tensions of women's spiritual journeys and celebrates the embodied nature of human life. In the story of the street household, Morrison reveals the social systems and economic models that have controlled women's bodies and supported an identification of woman as body" (Susan Corey Everson, "Toni Morrison's *Tar Baby*: A Resource for Feminist Theology," *Journal of Feminist Studies in Religion* Vol. 5 No. 2 <Fall, 1989, pp. 65-78>, p. 78).

comparative terms.[17] It may be evil to kill one's daughter, but slavery is more evil. Dwight N. Hopkins writes:

> The history of enslaved blacks in North America offers a fertile site for the development of a theology which originates out of a particular set of cultural expressions about beliefs, and, furthermore, can serve as a heuristic for all genres of theological methodology, especially liberation theologies.[18]

The dominant ethical system would not take this position. It will be hard to find anyone in the white community today who would say that slavery is more evil than killing one's own child. And even in the African-American community, it would not be easy to find people who will go on record to say this, particularly to a white person or in front of the white community. Of course, there are those who will go on record to agree with the ethics of *Beloved*. Nicole Wilkinson writes: "Sethe seems to have been correct that this was the way out."[19] But for most people and for Toni Morrison, fantasy provided the opportunity to make this statement without social recrimination. Fantasy is a genre of subversion. Toni Morrison probably would not make such a statement outright, for instance, at Princeton University, when she is teaching a Freshman Seminar. But the genre of fantasy allows her to say things that would otherwise be outrageous by the standards of dominant societal mores. This applies to the African-American community as a whole. Fantasy allows the African-American community to express internally scripturalized position that slavery is the greatest evil to the African-American community.[20]

In a sense, therefore, *Beloved* as the fantastic genre element represents a scripturalizing (and moralizing) tendency to emphasize that slavery is the greatest evil in the society, more evil than the worst crime that a person can imagine.[21] Mother killing her own daughter probably would come close to the worst crime that a sane person could commit. Sethe is not described as insane in the story. She is described as a normal mother. She knew what she did and why she did it. Sethe had no regrets about killing her daughter to prevent her from falling into the hands of white slave owners[22]. She did not have any regret when

---

[17] Valerie Smith, *Self-Discovery and Authority in Afro-American Narrative* (Cambridge: Harvard University Press, 1987), p. 122.
[18] Dwight N. Hopkins, "Theological Methods and Cultural Studies," p. 163.
[19] Wilkinson, "The Getting of Names," p. 243.
[20] Oprah Winfrey said in the BBC interview: "What it would take to have that kind of courage? To feel her resentment and abhorrence of slavery so much so that she would kill her own children and try to kill herself rather than be taken back into slavery?" ("Oprah Winfrewy and Beloved," BBC News interview, Friday, March 5, 1999).
[21] Brian Finney, "Temporal Defamiliarization in Toni Morrison's *Beloved*," *Critical Essays on Toni Morrison's* Beloved, ed. Barbara H. Solomon (New York: G. K. Hall & Co., 1998, pp. 104-116), p. 115.
[22] Morrison, *Beloved*, p. 194.

she did it, and she did not have any regrets eighteen years later[23] even with constant memory of her act.[24] Sethe's morality was a constant.

In this regard, Emily Griesinger completely misses the point. Griesinger writes: "The central issue in the novel is Sethe's redemption. Can she forgive herself for killing Beloved...?"[25] Also, Griesinger describes Sethe's redemption as "to do justice to the burden of guilt that Sethe carries after killing Beloved...."[26] The reason that Griesinger falls into this error is because she sees "Christian" as oppositional to "African." Describing the Christian service of Baby Suggs in the Clearing in the woods on Saturdays, Griesinger writes: "Here they dance, sing, shout, and cry in a manner some would find heathenish and pagan, more African than Chrstian."[27] Griesinger must not have been to many African-American Christian worship services. Not only does she condemn the manner of African-American Christian religiosity in effect, she faults the religiosity in *Beloved* as not being Christian because there is not a call to accept Jesus Christ as Lord and be born again and an emphasis on holy Christian living.[28] There are many white Christian churches, even those which profess to be evangelical, which will not emphasize these points on a weekly basis. Thus, the dialectic between "African" and "Christian" which Griesinger sets up does not work.

But the most serous problem is that Griesinger completely misses the point of *Beloved* and its notion of (earthly) redemption being emphasized in distinctively African-American terms based on the African-American experience. Griesinger errs in that she tries to understand (earthly) redemption described in *Beloved* in terms of spiritual salvation and after-life redemption so emphasized in evangelical Christianity and normative Roman Catholicism.[29] It is not faith that brings about spiritual salvation and heavenly forgiveness that Sethe is focusing on as a character in *Beloved*. Toni Morrison is not interested in a theological exposition about spiritual salvation in Heaven. Rather, Morrison and her character Sethe in *Beloved* focus on individual and communal redemption in the earthly realm and in the physical world. A more constructive way to approach the concept of earthly redemption and salvation in the physical realm that Toni Morrison and her novel *Beloved* focus on is to understand this in

---

[23] Morrison, *Beloved*, p. 236.
[24] Carol Iannone describes this attitude of Sethe as "defiant" (Iannone, "Toni Morrison's Career," p. 63).
[25] Emily Griesinger, "Why Baby Sugges, Holy, Quit Preaching the Word: Redemption and Holiness in Toni Morrison's *Beloved*," *Christianity and Literature* Vol. 50, No. 4 (Summer, 2001, pp. 689-702), p. 689.
[26] Griesinger, "Why Baby Suggs," p. 691.
[27] Griesinger, "Why Baby Suggs," p. 693.
[28] Griesinger, "Why Baby Suggs," pp. 692-295.
[29] Griesinger, "Why Baby Suggs," p. 699.

terms of Liberation Theology[30] that is dominant in Latin American countries, characterized by oppression, particularly at the hand of Communist regimes. Slavery was the greatest evil during the time of slavery, and it was the greatest evil even when it ceased to exist, represented in white oppression of the people of color. There is no moral ambivalence about slavery. There is no crime or action that is more evil than slavery itself. This scripturalizing tendency is embodied in the character of Beloved.

Toni Morrison's *Beloved* represents a scripture that pushes a moral value system in which slavery is the greatest evil. In this regard, the literary narrative can be seen as counter-cultural or subversive of dominant culture. Beloved as the fantastic character is at the center of the subversive message, but the whole plot of the story works toward that end. The fact that the African-American community of Ohio in the narrative concludes that slavery was more evil and exonerates Sethe of killing her daughter[31] is instructive to this particular scripturalizing tendency. Even Paul D, who abandons Sethe after finding out that she killed her own daughter, comes back and reunites with Sethe.[32] Not only does Paul D recognizes Sethe's right to kill her daughter to protect her from slavery, he is found in the narrative praising Sethe and her virtuous character.[33] The plot (especially towards the end of the novel) and other characters in the story all point toward the scripturalizing tendency in the narrative to emphasize that slavery is the greatest evil in the world and no evil can compare to it. In this regard, Nicole Wilkinson's point is important: "Texts and readers have real and not only literary pasts; both bear scars from the conflicted history of their relatedness."[34]

Beloved, therefore, points to redemption. Beloved is redemption for the African-American community because she helps them realize that slavery is the greatest evil. There is no crime or sin greater than slavery. Beloved is redemption because African-Americans who have committed any crime under slavery – even as serious as killing one's own daughter–is exonerated for the crime because slavery is the greatest evil. Beloved is redemption because it unites African-Americans fragmented by the evils of slavery and its evil policy of divide and conquer[35] that cause members of the community to blame other

---

[30] See Wilkinson, "The Getting of Names," pp. 242-243. Also, see James A. Noel, "The Post-Modern Location of Black Religion: Texts and Temporalities in Tension," *Changing Conversations: Religious Reflection & Cultural Analysis*, ed. Dwight N. Hopkins and Sheila Greeve Danney (New York: Routledge, 1996, p. 79-99), p. 81.
[31] Morrison, *Beloved*, p. 307.
[32] Morrison, *Beloved*, p. 310.
[33] Morrison, *Beloved*, p. 322.
[34] Wilkinson, "The Getting of Names," p. 245.
[35] Vincent Wimbush states that slave owners intentionally disrupted open communication of protest among slaves and thus slaves used the open language of the Bible to cloak their protest and discontent (Vincent Wimbush, "The Bible and African-Americans: An

members for the evils of slavery and other wrongs perpetrated against the community by white slave owners. Beloved represents a fantastic subversion of dominant culture[36] which places blame on African-American individuals and the African-American community for crimes committed by African-Americans as the result of the evils of slavery and discrimination against the people of color.[37] Thus, this work of fantasy represents a functional pushing of the norms of society as perceived by the dominant culture. Whereas the dominant culture refuses to prioritize the idea that slavery and discrimination against the people of color are the greatest evil, this African-American scripture stands up for the African-American community and defines what is the greatest evil for the African-American community. Thus, by providing the African-American worldview in regards to the African-American historical experience, Toni Morrison's *Beloved* is scripturalized with distinctively African-American interests. In this regard, Dwight N. Hopkins' conclusions are significant:

> My claim is that enslaved African American experience–as religious culture– can serve as an intentional location where theological method can learn from cultural studies. Theological method–how one goes about studying convictions and practices about the most ultimate meaning in life–can no longer consider itself as located at a metaphysical height that assures neutrality. Cultural studies, especially social sciences, presents a bounteous opportunity to strip away, map, and reconfigure the multiple layers of theology.[38]

Outline of an Interpretative History," *Stony the Road We Trod*, ed. Cain Hope Felder <Minneapolis: Fortress, 1991, pp. 81-97>, p. 82).

[36] Griesinger acknowledges: "Morrison has said that many critics are unprepared to understand her work because they have no appreciation of the culture out of which she writes" (Griesinger, "Why Baby Suggs," p. 700).

[37] Ann-Janine Morey writes: "Too often, white liberals try to demonstrate their racial generosity by insisting that color doesn't make a difference, and that aside from the natural accident of color we have in common our humanity. Black writers know better. Color has made every difference in the world to the black American, and it continues to do so despite others' good intentions. To be colored body was to be under sentence of death, and Morrison does not flinch from trying to communicate what it means to be living color in a racist world" (Ann-Janine Morey, "Toni Morrison and the Color of Life," *The Christian Century* 105 <November 16, 1988, pp. 1039-1042>, p. 1041).

[38] Dwight N. Hopkins, "Theological Method and Cultural Studies," p. 177.

Bibliography

Bailey, Randall C., and Jacquelyn Grant (Editors). *The Recovery of Black Presence: An Interdisciplinary Exploration* (Essays in Honor of Dr Charles B. Copher). Nashville: Abingdon Press, 1997.

Everson, Susan Corey. "Toni Morrison's *Tar Baby*: A Resource for Feminist Theology." *Journal of Feminist Studies in Religion* Vol. 5 No. 2 (Fall, 1989), pages 65-78.

Felder, Cain Hope (Editor). *Stony the Road We Trod*. Minneapolis: Fotress, 1991.

Griesinger, Emily. "Why Baby Suggs, Holy, Quit Preaching the Word: Redemption and Holiness in Toni Morrison's *Beloved*." *Christianity and Literature* Vol. 50, No. 4 (Summer 2001), pp. 689-702.

Grewal, Gurleen. *Circles of Sorrow, Lines of Struggle*. Baton Rouge: Louisiana State University Press, 1998.

Gross, Seymour L., and John Edward Hardy (Editors). *Images of the Negro in American Literature*. Chicago: The University of Chicago Press, 1966.

Harding, Wendy, and Jacky Martin. *A World of Difference: An Inter-Cultural Study of Toni Morrison's Novels*. Westport: Greenwood Press, 1994.

Hopkins, Dwight N., and Sheila Greeve Daveney (Editors). *Changing Conversations: Religious Reflection & Cultural Analysis*. New York: Routledge, 1996.

Iannone, Carol. "Toni Morrison's Career." *Commentary* Vol. 84 No. 6 (December 1987), pages 59-63.

Jackson, Rosemary. *Fantasy, the Literature of Subversion*. London: Methuen, 1981.

Major, Clarence. *The Dark and Feeling: Black American Writers and Their Work*. New York: The Third Press, 1974.

Mays, Benjamin E. *The Negro's God as Reflected in His Literature*. New York: Russell & Russell, 1938.

Morey, Ann-Janine. "Toni Morrison and the Color of Life." *The Christian Century* 105 (November 16, 1988), pages 1039-1042.

Morrison, Toni. "Behind the Making of *The Black Book*." *Black World* 23 (February 1974), pages 86-90.

Morrison, Toni. *Beloved: A Novel*. New York: Vintage Books, 2004.

Morrison, Toni. "Rootedness: The Ancestor as Foundation" in *Black Women Writers (1950-1980): A Critical Evaluation*. Edited by Mari Evans. Garden City: Anchor Press/Doubleday, 1984.

Oppenheimer, Paul. *Evil and the Demonic: A New Theory of Monstrous Behavior*. New York: New York University Press, 1996.

Otten, Terry. *The Crime of Innocence in the Fiction of Toni Morrison*. Columbia: University of Missouri Press, 1989.

Petesch, Donald A. *A Spy in the Enemy's Country: The Emergence of Modern Black Literature*. Iowa City: University of Iowa Press, 1989.

Rody, Caroline. *The Daughter's Return: African-American and Caribbean Women's Fiction of History*. New York: Oxford University Press, 2001.

Smith, Valerie. *Self-Discovery and Authority in Afro-American Narrative*. Cambridge: Harvard University Press, 1987.

Solomon, Barbara H. (Editor). *Critical Essays on Toni Morrison's* Beloved. New York: G. K. Hall & Co., 1998.

Thomas, H. Nigel. *From Folklore to Fiction: A Study of Folk Heroes and Rituals in the Black American Novel*. New York: Greenwood Press, 1988.

Todorov, Tzvetan. *The Fantastic: A Structural Approach to a Literary Genre*. Translated by Richard Howard. Ithaca: Cornell University Press, 1975.

Wilkinson, Nicole. "'The Getting of Names': Anti-Intertextuality and the Unread Bible in Toni Morrison's *Song of Solomon* and *Beloved*." *Semeia* 69/70 (1995), pages 235-246.

About the Author

Professor Heerak Christian Kim is Visiting Professor of Biblical Studies at Asia Evangelical College and Seminary in Bangalore, India. Professor Kim is a leading expert on the Jewish Second Temple and Late Antiquity. He was a Lady Davis Fellow of Israel in 1996-97 and a Raoul Wallenberg Scholar for Democracy and Human Rights at the Hebrew University of Jerusalem in 1995-96. Professor Kim is regularly invited by leading international conferences. Most recently, he was invited by the International Organization for the Study of the Old Testament (IOSOT) held in Slovenia, Canada's Global Conference on 9/11 held in Montreal, and 2007 International Meeting of the Society of Biblical Literature in Vienna, Austria. His numerous publications include *Key Signifier as Literary Device: Its Definition and Function in Literature and Media* (Edwin Mellen Press, 2006), *Jerusalem Tradition in the Late Second Temple Period: Diachronic and Synchronic Developments Surrounding Psalms of Solomon 11* (University Press of America, 2007), and *Jewish Law and Identity: Academic Essays* (The Hermit Kingdom Press, 2005)